Casino Comps

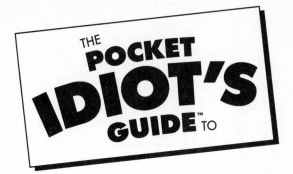

Casino Comps

by David Apostolico

ALPHA

A member of Penguin Group (USA) Inc.

ALPHA BOOKS

Published by the Penguin Group

Penguin Group (USA) Inc., 375 Hudson Street, New York, New York 10014, USA

Penguin Group (Canada), 90 Eglinton Avenue East, Suite 700, Toronto, Ontario M4P 2Y3, Canada (a division of Pearson Penguin Canada Inc.)

Penguin Books Ltd., 80 Strand, London WC2R 0RL, England

Penguin Ireland, 25 St. Stephen's Green, Dublin 2, Ireland (a division of Penguin Books Ltd.)

Penguin Group (Australia), 250 Camberwell Road, Camberwell, Victoria 3124, Australia (a division of Pearson Australia Group Pty. Ltd.)

Penguin Books India Pvt. Ltd., 11 Community Centre, Panchsheel Park, New Delhi—110 017, India

Penguin Group (NZ), 67 Apollo Drive, Rosedale, North Shore, Auckland 1311, New Zealand (a division of Pearson New Zealand Ltd.)

Penguin Books (South Africa) (Pty.) Ltd., 24 Sturdee Avenue, Rosebank, Johannesburg 2196, South Africa

Penguin Books Ltd., Registered Offices: 80 Strand, London WC2R 0RL, England

International Standard Book Number: 978-1-59257-653-1
Library of Congress Catalog Card Number: 2007930852

09 08 07   8 7 6 5 4 3 2 1

Interpretation of the printing code: The rightmost number of the first series of numbers is the year of the book's printing; the rightmost number of the second series of numbers is the number of the book's printing. For example, a printing code of 07-1 shows that the first printing occurred in 2007.

Printed in the United States of America

Note: This publication contains the opinions and ideas of its author. It is intended to provide helpful and informative material on the subject matter covered. It is sold with the understanding that the author and publisher are not engaged in rendering professional services in the book. If the reader requires personal assistance or advice, a competent professional should be consulted.

The author and publisher specifically disclaim any responsibility for any liability, loss, or risk, personal or otherwise, which is incurred as a consequence, directly or indirectly, of the use and application of any of the contents of this book.

Most Alpha books are available at special quantity discounts for bulk purchases for sales promotions, premiums, fund-raising, or educational use. Special books, or book excerpts, can also be created to fit specific needs.

For details, write: Special Markets, Alpha Books, 375 Hudson Street, New York, NY 10014.

Contents

Appendixes

Introduction

The number of casinos in the United States has increased greatly. While Atlantic City and Vegas are still the casino capitals of the United States, casinos can be found throughout the country. From Indian reservations to riverboats to racinos, everyone is competing for customers. Gamblers have never had so many choices to choose from, yet the comp system remains a mystery to many.

With so many casinos interested in your action, it pays to understand the comp system and how you can get your share. Bet smart and get credit for your action.

Using This Book

In addition to the main text, this book includes sidebars, each with a distinctive visual cue:

High Roller Talk

These sidebars include definitions of casino terms and slang.

Jackpot

These sidebars give you tips to help you get the most comps for your play.

Busted

These describe pitfalls to avoid in a casino.

The Royal Flush

These provide inside glimpses of casino myths, legends, and lore.

Acknowledgments

I would like to thank my agent Sheree Bykofsky for hooking me up with the great people at Alpha Books. I also would like to thank the following individuals who made a big impact on this book: Paul Dinas and Janette Lynn at Alpha and Ginny Bess Munroe.

Finally, my biggest thanks and gratitude go out to my wife Cindy and my boys Evan, Ryan, and Derek, who encourage, support, and provide never-ending inspiration. Comps are nice but they don't beat the comforts of home.

Trademarks

All terms mentioned in this book that are known to be or are suspected of being trademarks or service marks have been appropriately capitalized. Alpha Books and Penguin Group (USA) Inc. cannot attest to the accuracy of this information. Use of a term in this book should not be regarded as affecting the validity of any trademark or service mark.

Get Paid to Play

In this Chapter

- What is a comp?
- Who can qualify?
- There's no such thing as a free lunch
- It doesn't matter if you win or lose
- Don't play for comps

Gambling is big business, and casinos want yours. In the popular gambling cities Las Vegas and Atlantic City alone, there are countless casinos hoping you will walk in their doors to pull a lever, throw the dice, or lay down your cards.

How do they get you in their doors? High-profile entertainment, top-rate restaurants, and an inviting or themed atmosphere are just a few ways casinos lure you in.

With the expansion of gambling to locations across the country, including riverboats and Indian reservations, the industry is thriving. The number of casinos in the United States rose by 19 percent between 2001 and 2006. But without attracting and retaining players, casinos cannot survive, which is good news for you. Keeping you, the customer, will always be a high priority for casinos, and nothing brings in and keeps more loyal customers than a program of good rewards for players, also known as comps.

While the casinos will promote rewards programs and make memberships easily available, they will not readily share how to earn comps and they certainly won't advise how to rack up the most comps at the least cost. That is what this book is for.

Unraveling the Mystery

Most casinos offer player-rewards programs or *comps*. It is like the frequent-flier programs the airlines offer, but instead of earning miles by flying a particular airline and redeeming the miles for an airline ticket, you earn points by playing your favorite games and can redeem points for drinks, meals, chips, and even hotel rooms. How do you begin, you ask? Keep reading.

High Roller Talk

The word **comp** is an abbreviation for complimentary and refers to those freebies ranging from free meals to free hotel rooms that casinos use to reward their customers. It can also be used in a verb form as in "I got comped for dinner and a show."

Getting Started

Entering a casino can be an overwhelming experience. The sounds, chatter, hustle, and bustle can lead to stimulation overload. If you've never played before, it can be nerve-racking to sit down to a table game feeling that the eyes of all of the other players are scrutinizing you. Keeping your focus on your game of choice will require your full attention without worrying about getting comped.

The good news is that there is absolutely nothing to worry about. Casino employees from dealers and floor people are all there to help you out. They want you to play and are happy to provide you with any guidance you need.

There is more good news. Casinos want you earning comps. Yes, that's right. They know savvy players expect comps so they make them readily available. Ask any employee where you can sign up for a player's card, and you'll have one within minutes.

You'll find a window where there are employees more than happy to help you out. All you have to do is provide your name, address, and e-mail address and your card will be printed out on the spot.

Make sure you let the employee know what games you are interested in playing. Most casinos will have one card that can be used for all casino games while some will have separate cards for games like slots or poker. So make sure you have the right card before you start play.

Next, inquire if there are any promotional incentives for signing up. Casinos frequently offer promotions such as a coupon book or a roll of quarters for joining. Others will offer things such as free T-shirts, entries to sweepstakes, and even match play where the casino will match your bet dollar for dollar up to a specified amount.

Of course, they are not going to mention any incentives advertised in local newspapers or magazines. So check out those first. Many of these will contain coupons for things such as free meals, coffee cups, or T-shirts.

It's a Business

Casinos don't offer comps out of the niceness of their hearts. There is a method to their generosity. Comps are earned based on a theoretical loss. Casinos don't track whether you win or lose, but how much you wager.

Casino games all provide a house edge. There will be plenty of variances and some players will win—some players will lose. The house doesn't care who wins or loses as long as money is wagered. Over time, the house is going to win no matter what.

Theoretically, every individual will lose over time if he continues to wager enough. In reality, no one player will lose money at the exact rate of the house edge. So casinos are only concerned with your theoretical loss.

A Simple Formula

There is a basic formula casinos use as a starting point in determining how comps are earned. The purpose of the formula is to get as good an estimate as possible of your theoretical loss. The formula looks something like this:

(Your Average Bet) × (The Hours You've Played) × (Wagers per Hour) × (House Advantage) = Your Theoretical Loss

Say, for example, that you play roulette for five hours and average $10 a bet. On average, you can get 40 spins of the roulette wheel in per hour and the house edge is approximately 5 percent. Thus, we can determine your theoretical loss for this session as follows:

$10 × 5 hours × 40 wagers per hour × .05 house edge = $100.

In your five-hour session of roulette, you have incurred a $100 theoretical loss. It doesn't matter if you've actually won or lost. Because casinos deal in such high volume, all of the individual theoretical losses will come close to approximating the total actual loss even though each individual's wins and losses will vary greatly.

So what does this mean? If you have a $100 theoretical loss, the casino isn't going to turn around and hand you your $100 back. That would be a zero-sum game for the casino and they would be out of business in a hurry.

Instead, casinos generally will reward players with comps equal to 10 to 40 percent of their theoretical losses. We'll refer back to the basic formula in future chapters. For now, keep in mind that each of the factors mentioned (average bet, hours played, wagers per hour, and house advantage) is a variable that you have some ability to manipulate in your favor.

 Jackpot

You don't have to be a big shot to receive a comp. No matter what your game or how much your wager, casinos want your business and are willing to pay for it.

Not Just for High Rollers

Go into any casino and the super–high rollers are going to have their every whim catered to. A personal concierge will be at their beck and call making sure every comfort is met and every need is satisfied. The finest food and drink will be available around the clock, private jets, and top-of-the-line penthouse suites at their disposal. Of course, that stuff ain't cheap. But there aren't a lot of players in that stratosphere.

Casinos spend billions of dollars a year and, while you would think it is spent on the high rollers, most of that money is going to the average player. Casinos can't make money without the business of all the average bettors. They are the bread and butter of the industry and their business is invaluable to the casino's bottom line. Anyone who is willing to play can qualify for comps. At the lower levels, it may just take a little longer to rack up some freebies.

Keep in mind the formula. If a high roller loses $10 million in a weekend, the casino can provide a lot of comps.

If you suffer a $100 theoretical loss, a $20 comp represents 20 percent, which is a better return than our high-roller loser.

You Have to Pay to Play

Nobody likes a freeloader and casinos are no different. If you are not there to wager, then don't expect freebies. Go for the food, shows, and entertainment and have fun, but expect to pay for all of your needs just like you would if you were out anywhere else.

Comps are saved for the players as a way of rewarding them for their action as well as encouraging them to keep playing. If you don't feel like spending $5 for a drink at the bar, then take the $5 to a slot machine and order a drink while you're playing. The drink's free and you may win something with the $5. If you were going to spend the $5 on a drink anyway, you are getting a *freeroll* at the slot machine.

High Roller Talk

When a player is playing with the casino's money, it may be referred to as a **freeroll**.

Play to Win

One of the biggest misconceptions surrounding comps is that you have to lose a lot of money in order to qualify. Nothing could be further from the truth. Let's face it. The overwhelming majority of casino games are all tilted in the casino's favor.

Don't misinterpret that. The casinos aren't cheating. They don't need to. The games provide a built-in advantage for the house. Depending on the game and how you play, the house edge can range from less than one percent to a percentage in the high teens. The only exceptions are in blackjack and poker.

In blackjack, players can count cards and adjust their bets accordingly to tilt the edge in their favor. Casinos, of course, look unfavorably upon that and will take great measures to prevent it. Using numerous decks and reshuffling, Casinos frequently limit a player's ability to count cards. Even if a player does find success, it's within a casino's right to prohibit a card counter from playing. Poker is the only casino game where the players compete against each other instead of the house. The casinos don't care who wins as they take a cut, or rake, out of each pot. Thus, they can't lose.

In every other game, the casinos have an edge so they don't care who wins and loses in the short term. They know that as long as they have steady customers and action, they will make plenty of money in the long term. Whether you win or lose, casinos want your play.

In fact, you could even make the argument that casinos are more likely to reward winners than losers. Winners have money the house doesn't want going to a rival casino. The bottom line is that casinos look at how much you wager and for how long, not the outcome of those wagers. So if you're going to gamble, play to win and don't be shy about asking for comps no matter what the result.

Play Within Your Means

Before we go any further, take a minute and reflect on this chapter. It's exciting to know that you can earn comps for doing something you enjoy. However, let's not lose sight of the fact that the great majority of the games offered are losing propositions for the players.

Gaming can be a fun social activity for many, and it can provide hours of enjoyment. Look at it as a recreational activity such as golf or shopping.

Most importantly, look at comps as an added bonus for something you enjoy doing anyway. It's like going to your favorite coffee shop where you get one free cup of coffee for every ten you buy. If you didn't like coffee, you would never buy ten cups just to get a free one.

> **Busted**
>
> Play with your head and not over your head. A free meal isn't worth losing more than you can afford.

Similarly, you should never wager money just for the comps. That's a losing proposition and could be a sign of a bigger problem. This book is written for the great majority of players who play for entertainment purposes and enjoy the exciting and relaxing atmosphere of a casino.

Unfortunately, a small majority of players will turn into problem gamblers. If you think you may have a problem, please see Appendix C for help in determining if you have a problem and where you can get help.

Manage Your Bankroll

The best way to avoid piling up losses is to initiate a proper money-management system. First, set aside a separate account of discretionary funds that you absolutely do not need for any other purpose. This should be money that is for entertainment purposes only.

A certain amount of each paycheck could go to this account for gambling or other entertainment activities. If you lose this money, do not spend any more until you can replenish this account from future earnings.

Next, keep accurate and up-to-date records of all your wins and losses. This will help you keep your gaming in perspective and may come in handy come tax time. If your losses are more than you like, then it may be best to take some time off away from the casino and use that discretionary income for other entertainment activities.

> **Jackpot**
>
> While everyone should consult their own accountant, many gamblers view comps as a rebate on their money wagered and, thus, as not taxable.

There will be a lot of variance in your play. Sometimes you will win and sometimes you will lose. When you win, enjoy it. Treat yourself to something special whether it's a nice meal or a new shirt.

Don't spend it all, though. Put a large chunk right back into that separate account. Losing days are sure to come so be prepared.

The Least You Need to Know

- Comps are available to anyone who bellies up to a table or slot machine and wagers her hard earned money.
- Comps are based on a theoretical loss, taking into account the amount you wager, the length of time you play, and the house edge of the game.

- Losers aren't rewarded more than winners so don't be shy about asking for comps no matter how well you do.

- Play within your means. Comps are a nice bonus if you enjoy playing for recreational purposes but never gamble for the purpose of receiving a comp.

Chapter 2

Get in the Game

In This Chapter

- Before you go
- Promos, coupons, and other goodies
- Signing up
- Don't be afraid to ask

Now that you know that if you are going to play, you should be getting comped, it's time to get started. In this chapter, we take a look at what you need to know before you wager your next nickel.

The time to think about comps is before you start playing, not afterward. If you wait until you've already played, it may be too late to get rewarded for all of your previous action.

Incentives Before the Comps

Before you even walk in the door, your preparation should begin. There's plenty you can do to save yourself time and money. In today's world, information is readily available from numerous sources so take advantage of all of them. A good place to start is the websites of potential casinos you want to visit. Any ongoing promotions will usually be listed. There are many outside sources to research as well. A few of the more valuable ones are listed in Appendix C.

Find a Good Host

Call ahead of time (to the casino's 1-800 number, of course) and ask to speak to a *casino host*. They will be the most knowledgeable people when it comes to comps. It's a common mistake to believe that hosts only talk to high rollers.

> **High Roller Talk** _____
>
> Employees whose job it is to look out for the needs of casino customers are called **casino hosts**. They are there to help with everything related to a guest's relationship with the casino.

In fact, casino hosts are readily available to speak with anyone. When you meet them, let them know your history and what you plan on playing when you get there. Ask if you can give them a call if you're down.

Be honest about the assessment of your play. If you're a $1-slot player, don't say you play blackjack for $500 a hand. Discuss your needs and find out

what they can offer you. Ask how comps are calcu-
lated in the game you want to play and if there are
any current promotional offers. Find out about the
amenities you are interested in and if anything can
be done for you.

Casino hosts have discretion to offer comps above
and beyond what you earn on your card. By intro-
ducing yourself, you can let them know about your
past play at other casinos. If you have a premium
card from a different casino (which is earned with
a lot of play), you are likely to be offered at least a
free room right off the bat.

Jackpot

When planning your trip,
check out the websites of the
casinos that you are planning on visiting.
Often, you will find room and package
deals available only on the Internet.

Even if you are new, ask if there are any special
deals for new players. Follow up with this host once
you arrive. Have someone call him while you are
playing. This serves two purposes. First, it may
take a while for your host to arrive, so you can
keep playing. Second, when your host does arrive,
he'll witness you playing.

Of course, if you're alternating between 25-cent
slot machines and $1 slot machines, make sure
you're playing the $1 machine when she comes.

Any comp you may get from a casino host will be in addition to points earned from your play, so there's nothing to lose by asking.

The Thrill of the Find

Coupons are available in many places. Local newspapers, phone books, magazines, and flyers all contain discount coupons. If you are going to Atlantic City or Las Vegas, look for one of the many local weekly newspapers. Most of them are free and can be found on street corners in both cities. When you check in to your room, often you'll be given a magazine or book containing coupons or you'll find one in the room. If you don't, ask the concierge or the check-in desk attendant if they have any magazines, books, or newspapers containing information on local restaurants and nightlife. Specifically, ask if they have a free fun book, which may contain coupons for everything from food and drinks to gaming.

Even if you are not staying in the casino's hotel, don't be shy about asking the concierge.

If you're diligent, you'll be amazed at the savings you'll find. Ask housekeepers and cab drivers if they know of any deals around town. People that work close to the casino business (and who work for tips) have a lot of secrets that they are happy to share. I've been turned on to more than a few bargain dinners in Las Vegas this way.

The Royal Flush

When Pennsylvania's first casinos opened in 2006, a few glitches were to be expected. At one racetrack casino, the glitch was glaring. A player hit a six-figure jackpot at a slot machine only to be told that it was a mistake due to an employee testing the machine's payout. Even though the casino had some legal ground on its side, it finally relented and paid the customer after the negative publicity proved to be too much. This story illustrates how critical it is for casinos to maintain great customer relations.

Matchplay

Many casinos offer first-time visitors such good-ies as $5 in credit on a slot machine or a matchplay coupon for a table game. The matchplay coupon works just like real money, but you have to spend it at the table. If you win, it's yours to keep.

For example, you receive a $5 matchplay coupon good for any even-money bet (i.e, a bet that pays 1-1 on the amount wagered). You walk over to the roulette table and put a $5 chip plus the $5 coupon down on red. The casino has matched your $5 bet with $5 of its own. If red wins, you'll win $10. If it doesn't, you've only lost $5.

Other gaming coupons may offer bonus dollars such as a 7-5 coupon. With this one, that same $5 bet as above will now be the equivalent of $7. Not quite as lucrative as the matchplay but still worth playing.

Even if you're purely a slot player, don't turn down a free coupon for a table game. The even-money bets require little or no knowledge and the dealers or other patrons will generally provide any guidance you need. Don't be shy about placing just the one coupon-enhanced bet and then walking away.

Casinos make their money by having a small advantage that adds up over time. You have the advantage with a matchplay bet. You might not win every time, but if you consistently take advantage of these promotions, you'll come out ahead on these bets over time.

Busted

Slot machines have the worst odds in a casino and the cheapest slot machines usually pay out the least.

Promotions

Casinos frequently offer promotions such as drawings and giveaways. Some of these will require no work on your part to enter. For instance, some poker rooms will offer hourly prizes for everyone playing who has provided their player's cards. Hats, T-shirts, or even jackets could be given away.

Other bigger drawings (such as cars and cash) typically won't require any play at all, but may be located in a part of the casino you don't pass. Ask about any promotions so you can enter. These are a long shot but someone has to win.

A Fun Reason to Check the Mail

More than just bills come in the mail. If you have a player's card, you are sure to be on the casino's mailing list. This is a great way to keep abreast of all the latest offerings. Casinos will frequently mail incentives to their mailing lists including package deals on rooms, food, and entertainment. From discounted and free rooms to two-for-one meals, the mailings will run the gamut.

Even if you are strictly a small-stakes player, you will receive offers even if they are for mid-week. Yes, some (but certainly not all) of these offers will be open to anybody but by being on the mailing list, you won't miss it. Also, many of these offers are limited in quantity so you'll get an early crack at them.

Don't feel shy about sharing your e-mail address, either. Sending e-mails is a cost-effective way for casinos to keep in touch and send you up-to-the-minute incentives and package deals.

Casinos often run special events that are strictly limited to those holding player's cards. Everything from private parties to gaming events such as slot, poker, or blackjack tournaments where you can win real money will be offered.

Jackpot _____

When signing up for a player's card, inquire if there are any free gifts or bonus points available.

Before You Play

Never play without a player's card—whether it's a new casino or an old one. If you have a card, there's no excuse not to use it. You may think you're only going to play for a minute and it's not worth it. Of course, that minute session could turn into an hour and before you know it, you haven't gotten any credit for your play.

Even if you are only going to put the two quarters that are burning a hole in your pocket into a slot machine, you just never know. Those quarters may bring a lot more in wins. For example, say you play those 2 quarters from your pocket and end up winning 20 quarters. Instead of walking away, you play some more with those 20 quarters.

You win some more and lose some more and after an hour of spins, you walk away down those two quarters. All that play for that past hour would have earned you points if you had bothered to swipe your card. It doesn't matter that you played with your initial winnings.

Say you walk into a new casino for lunch with no intention of playing the games. You'd rather save your action for your home casino where you have a player's card. After lunch, though, the temptation to play some roulette proves too great. You don't bother with a card because you don't believe you'll be back any time soon. With every intention of just placing a couple of bets and being on your way, you end up on a winning streak and stay for a few hours.

While you walk out happy to be up $300, you have still lost money by not signing up for a player's card before you sat down. Those comp points can never be recouped. If you're going to play, make sure you have a card.

Plus, it doesn't hurt to have a player's card with another casino. You are sure to get some offers in the mail in the way of discounted rooms or other incentives.

And remember when you do sign up, you should be asking for any promotional bonuses just like you've learned. If I still haven't convinced you, consider this last fact. The casino industry is constantly changing and consolidating. Properties get bought and sold all the time. This new casino could soon be in the same corporate family as your home casino and your points could get consolidated. Never pass on an opportunity to earn points.

When in Doubt, Check It Out

Remember that casinos want your business, and they want to do everything they can to attract you and keep you. Promotions are all around in every form. Some are obvious and some not as much. Check everything out and ask questions.

Casinos can be an intimidating place with thousands of people running around all seemingly with a purpose. Most everyone is there to have a good time, and employees and patrons alike are all more than willing to help out if you have a question. Don't be intimidated into missing out.

The Royal Flush

Looking for the 13th floor? You won't find one in a casino. Thirteen being perceived as that most unlucky of numbers, most casinos choose to forego that floor going directly to floor 14 from 12 lest any superstitious customers find themselves stuck in room 1313.

The Least You Need to Know

- Do your homework ahead of time by calling the casino and researching on the Internet.
- Check local newspapers and magazines for coupons and promotions.
- Before you wager your first dollar, make sure you've signed up for a player's card.
- Never bet a nickel without making sure you're getting comp credit for your wager.

Chapter 3

The Comp Value of Each Game

In This Chapter

- Picking a game
- Slot and video games
- Blackjack: game of 21
- Craps: rolling the dice
- Spinning the wheel of roulette
- Poker: shuffle up and deal

No matter what your game of choice is, there are tricks to the trade for increasing your winning percentage and/or your comp value.

In this chapter, we dive into a detailed description of the comp value of each game. Before we get there, though, we're going to take some time to look at how each game differs in odds and skill so you can make an informed decision in choosing a game to your liking in order to maximize comps.

Which Game to Choose

When it comes to casino games, not all games are created equally. In fact, the odds of winning can vary greatly from game to game. Even what may seem like a small difference can prove large over time.

In addition, some games, such as most slot machines, require zero knowledge or skill at all. Others, such as blackjack, require you to make decisions, and if you can consistently make the right decision, you can lessen the house's advantage.

The comps you earn will depend on both the amount you bet and the game you choose. Games with a higher house edge will allow you to rack up comps quicker, but that's not a good tradeoff.

The Royal Flush

Contrary to what you might hear from some cynics, casinos don't cheat. They don't need to because every game played is in their favor.

In choosing a game, the most important consideration is to pick the one that you enjoy most. After all, you are supposed to be playing for fun. We're willing to bet, though, that the more money you win, the more fun you'll have.

A primer on the individual games offered in a casino is beyond the scope of this book. However, Appendix C lists additional resources for you to consult.

The House Edge

Casinos make their money by offering games that provide odds in their favor. For instance, if the *house edge* in a game is .05, then for every dollar wagered, the casino can expect to make five cents profit and the bettor can expect to lose five cents. Here are the approximate edges for the most popular casino games:

 High Roller Talk _____

The advantage the casino holds in any game is referred to as its edge or the **house edge**.

Game	House Edge
Blackjack	.005 (following basic strategy) .02 (not following basic strategy)
Roulette	.027–.0526 (varies by city, casino, and game)
Craps	.005 (pass line/full odds) .01 (knowledgeable player) .04 (uninformed player)

continues

continued

Game	House Edge
Baccarat	.012
Pai Gow Poker	.01 (knowledgeable player) .02 (uninformed player)
Slots	.03–.10 (approximate average numbers, although will vary greatly depending on state, casino, and machine)

Luck or Skill

As you can see from the chart, the advantage in some games depends on the player's actions. Player who know the correct decisions to make can decrease the house's advantage. In other games, there is nothing the player can do to lower the advantage.

Games such as roulette, baccarat, and slots require zero skill or knowledge. There are no decisions to be made that can alter your expected win rate. On the other hand, games such as blackjack, craps, and pai gow poker do require a baseline knowledge if you are going to lessen the casino's advantage. We hesitate to call those games skill, as no judgment is required. It's a matter of knowing how the game is played and which plays offer the best chances. Unless you are counting cards in blackjack, all of those games are still luck and the house will always have the edge. The only true skill game in a casino is poker. Poker is not played against the house but against other players. Not surprisingly, casinos offer the worst comps for poker but even those are improving.

The edge chart is included for two reasons. First, it illustrates the significant advantage the house possesses which is why it wants your business. Next, these edges are a critical factor when it comes to computing comps. If you recall our comp formula from Chapter 1, the house edge is a critical component.

It's important to know that for those games that require knowledge, the casino typically uses a percentage that is closer to the uninformed play rather than the informed play. The same formula is applied to all so for those in the know, they receive comp credits at a higher rate.

Spinning for Dollars and Comps

When it comes to slots, there's good news and bad news as far as comps are concerned. First, here's the bad news. Slots, on average, have the worst house edge of any game in the casino. The cheaper denomination machines usually have the biggest house edge. To make matters worse, there is nothing you can do to lessen that edge. The game is 100 percent luck and no amount of knowledge will improve your odds.

The good news is that because the house edge is so great, you can earn comps quicker. There are not a lot of secret tips to better comps with this one.

There is no guesswork involved when it comes time to record your action. You swipe your card before you begin playing and the machine will record your entire action. Bathroom breaks and phone calls won't help you.

There are a couple of things you can do to make life easier. If you play a lot, talk to a casino host to see if there is anything extra they can do. Also, take advantage of slot tournaments offered free of charge to valued customers. These are promotional events that typically offer the ultimate winner a substantial prize. Even if you don't win, it won't cost you anything and you may find yourself having more fun than in your typical gaming session.

Also, look into paying to enter a slot tournament. By doing so, you may be eligible for a discounted rate on a room. That discount may exceed the cost of the tournament in which case you are ahead of the game by entering the tournament.

A Better Alternative

If you are a hard-core slot player, consider trying video poker. Unlike slots, there are decisions to be made in video poker. However, it's an easy game to learn and once you gain a baseline knowledge, you can lower the house edge.

As you should know by now, if you can lower the house edge and get credit for a bigger house edge, you are ahead of the game when it comes to computing comps.

21 or Bust

Blackjack is a game where knowledge is king. Playing straightforward blackjack theory can decrease the house edge considerably and increase your comp win rate. First, let's take a look at a chart outlining basic blackjack strategy assuming the dealer has six or more decks:

Dealer Upcard

Your Hand	2	3	4	5	6	7	8	9	10	A
7	H	H	H	H	H	H	H	H	H	H
8	H	H	H	H	H	H	H	H	H	H
9	H	D	D	D	D	H	H	H	H	H
10	D	D	D	D	D	D	D	D	H	H
11	D	D	D	D	D	D	D	D	D	H
12	H	H	S	S	S	H	H	H	H	H
13	S	S	S	S	S	H	H	H	H	H
14	S	S	S	S	S	H	H	H	H	H
15	S	S	S	S	S	H	H	H	H	H
16	S	S	S	S	S	H	H	H	H	H
17	S	S	S	S	S	S	S	S	S	S
A,2	H	H	H	D	D	H	H	H	H	H
A,3	H	H	H	D	D	H	H	H	H	H
A,4	H	H	D	D	D	H	H	H	H	H
A,5	H	H	D	D	D	H	H	H	H	H
A,6	H	D	D	D	D	H	H	H	H	H
A,7	S	DS	DS	DS	DS	S	S	H	H	H

continues

Dealer Upcard (continued)

A,8	S	S	S	S	S	S	S	S	S	S
A,9	S	S	S	S	S	S	S	S	S	S
2,2	P	P	P	P	P	P	H	H	H	H
3,3	P	P	P	P	P	P	H	H	H	H
4,4	H	H	H	P	P	H	H	H	H	H
5,5	D	D	D	D	D	D	D	D	H	H
6,6	P	P	P	P	P	H	H	H	H	H
7,7	P	P	P	P	P	P	H	H	H	H
8,8	P	P	P	P	P	P	P	P	P	P
9,9	P	P	P	P	P	S	P	P	S	S
T,T	S	S	S	S	S	S	S	S	S	S
A,A	P	P	P	P	P	P	P	P	P	P
Dlr	2	3	4	5	6	7	8	9	10	A

Key:		
H = Hit	S = Stand	P = Split
D = Double (hit if not allowed)		
DS = Double (stand if not allowed)		

The chart looks imposing but is rather simple to follow. In fact, you will often find beginning players with a similar chart in front of them when they are playing.

The chart works like this. Say you are dealt a 5 and a 7, giving you a total of 12. The dealer has one down card, which you cannot see and a 9 for an up card. On the left hand column, find 12 which is your current hand. Then go across until you are under the 9 column which is the dealer's up card.

You'll find an H, which means that you should hit and take another card. You do and that card is a 3 giving you a total of 15.

Now, you find 15 on the left hand side and again go across until you are under the 9 since that is still the dealer's up card. Again, you see an H, so you take another card. This time you get a 2 giving you a grand total of 17. If you followed the same procedure, you will find an S this time, which means stand and don't take another card.

Basic blackjack strategy requires that you follow this strategy for every single hand. By playing this basic strategy, you cut the house edge to less than half a percent—which is significantly less than the 2 percent edge the house enjoys against players who don't follow this strategy. Because the house still has an edge, they don't mind if you have the chart with you.

Now, let's assume you also take your time making decisions and take a break or two for phone calls, the restroom, or just to stretch. By doing so, you are able to cut the amount of hands you play from the average of 60 per hour to around 50. You average $25 a bet and play for four hours.

> Let's look at how your knowledgeable play makes a difference in the comps earned. We can compute your theoretical loss using our formula: 25 (Your Average Bet) × 4 (The Hours You've Played) × 50 (Wagers per Hour) × .005 (House Advantage) = $25 (Your Theoretical Loss)

The bottom line, after four hours of knowledgeable play, you probably lost only $25.

Now, say the guy next to you also averaged $25 a bet for four hours but was playing without knowledge. His theoretical loss is:

$$(25) \times (4) \times (60) \times (.02) = \$120.$$

The particular casino you are playing at offers comps back at a rate of 30 percent of theoretical loss. The guy next to you has made $36 in comps. And because your comps will be based on the average play, not your superior play, you will make $36 in comps as well. By making small adjustments, like playing with some knowledge, you can potentially earn more in comps than your theoretical loss.

As far as the casino goes, they don't distinguish between who is playing with knowledge or not. Either way, they are still making money. So, you could even say that the nonknowledgeable player is subsidizing the knowledgeable player's comps.

Rolling the Dice

Craps is another game where knowledge is critical. Craps also can be a confusing game. With so many different bets going on and a crowd of players, it can be difficult to track individual play. There are a number of things as a player, however, that you can do to increase your comps.

First and foremost, become knowledgeable and find a game that offers correct odds. A knowledgeable player with full odds can lessen the house advantage from 4 percent to less than 1 percent. If you recall our formula for determining comps, the casino is likely to be offering comps as if the house edge were closer to 4 percent.

Here is a checklist of tips for maximizing comps when playing craps:

- Find a game with favorable odds—look for 5 times or better.

- Buy in for more than you intend to play with. Dealers and managers will record this number. Just make sure you have the discipline to play only with the amount you intended.

- Inquire if you get comp credit for your spread rather than individual bets. This will make a big difference.

- Make your first couple of bets larger than your average.

- Keep track of your play as far as time played and average amount wagered.

- When you are finished playing a session, check with the pit boss to make sure he has accurately recorded your play and you've earned the comp credits that you deserve.

The More, the Merrier

Baccarat and roulette can be fun games to play, but like slots, the house edge is large (the edge in roulette being bigger than baccarat) and the game is entirely luck.

Unlike slots, however, your action is not counted automatically. So buy in for more than you want to wager. Make your first few bets larger than average and play at a crowded table where the action will move a little slower. All of these things will help to increase your comp rate relative to your actual action.

 Jackpot

If you plan on entering a poker tournament, make plans well ahead of time. Host casinos usually will reserve a set amount of discounted rooms for players. However, because tournaments can attract hundreds of players, those discounted rooms get booked early.

All Skill, Few Comps

Poker has exploded in the last few years and casinos have taken note. Poker was a dying game before the advent of hidden cameras to see a player's cards brought it to television.

Prior to 2003, few casinos even had poker rooms and those that did had just a few tables or were in the process of shutting down their rooms. Poker players were looked upon as second-class citizens and the comps afforded them were commensurate to that status.

Since 2003, casinos have been in a rush to build new state-of-the-art poker rooms or expand and refurbish existing ones. The poker room is often now the nicest room in the house. Not so coincidentally, the comps have improved as well.

No Skin in the Game

Poker is a game of skill, but the casino still can't lose. Casinos provide the tables, dealers, chips, and cards, and the players play against each other. For its service, the casino takes a percentage out of each pot called a *rake*.

High Roller Talk

The money that the casino charges for each hand of poker is called the **rake**. It is usually a percentage, 5 to 10 percent, or flat fee that is taken from the pot after each round of betting.

A typical rake is 10 percent of the pot with a cap of $4. So the higher the stakes you play, the lesser the rake percentage. On average, approximately 25 poker hands can be dealt per hour per table. So at the highest stakes games, casinos are only making $100 per hour. Assuming 10 players per game, that's only $10 per player. Based on our formula, you can expect $1 to $4 back in comps.

That's fairly standard. At the lower stakes games, players can expect to earn 50 cents to a dollar per hour in comps while at the higher stakes, players may earn $4 an hour.

You're not going to get rich in comps by playing poker, but there are other incentives. Plenty of casinos allot a certain number of discounted rooms per night to their poker players. To qualify, you'll only need to play four hours a day or, if a major tournament is scheduled, play in that day's tournament.

In addition, many casinos host monthly poker tournaments with no entry fee for those customers who have logged the most hours at the tables that month.

The Least You Need to Know

- If you are playing a game that requires knowledge, make sure you are completely informed.
- Play to have fun but do it in a way as to maximize your comp value.
- Track your play and when you are done with a session, confirm that the pit boss has recorded your action correctly.
- If you play poker, call well ahead of time for discounted rooms.

Chapter 4

Secrets to Better Comps

In This Chapter

- Stick to one casino
- Playing the game
- You don't ask, you don't get

In this electronic age, much of the subjectivity surrounding comps has gone out the window. It has become easy for casinos to track each player's betting history or at least come up with a very good estimate. Comps are then accumulated based on rather standard formulas.

When it comes to comps, however, nothing is written in stone and not all gamblers are treated equally. The more savvy ones will maximize how much they receive for their playing dollars. In this chapter, we take a look at some inside tips to help you get the most bang for your gambling buck.

Find a Home

Casinos offer comps because they want your business. They reward loyalty. Comp points are earned and accumulated over time. So, if you are going to play, it makes sense to play where you want to be.

Make one casino your home and give it the largest chunk of your action. While you obviously want to choose a casino you like, you also want to choose one that rewards you adequately for your play and that provides the most useable comps for your level of play.

 Jackpot

Don't rely on superstitions. There's no such thing as a lucky casino or game for you. Be practical and objective and choose a casino that you like and that will provide the best comps for your play.

If you are new to the game, then take the time to check out various casinos and look at the following factors:

- What are the table limits on your favorite game? If you are a $5 blackjack player, don't play in a casino that only offers $5 blackjack a couple of hours a day. Find one that has plenty of tables at your limit when you want to play. Otherwise, you'll find yourself spreading your action out among too many casinos.

- Check out the amenities. It doesn't do you any good to rack up a lot of comps if you don't like any of the restaurants or the hotel rooms. Take the time to look around. Check out the menus and look at restaurant guides or reviews.

- How crowded is the casino? The most popular casino in town may not need to work as hard for your business.

- What will you get for your comp dollars? If you rack up comp dollars at the same rate at two different casinos, you may want to consider the casino with hotel rooms for $99 a night as opposed to the one with rooms priced at $249.

We're sure you'll have some personal factors of your own to add to this list. Once you do, measure everything up and try to find that one casino that is most suitable to your needs.

Be Realistic

If you are going to play, you should get the most comps that you can. However, you still need to be realistic. Don't walk in and play three hands of $5 blackjack and expect to be showered with freebies. There's nothing wrong with playing $5 blackjack, and if that's the game that fits your budget, by all means stick with it. Just temper your expectations. Do all the things outlined in this book and you will get your fair share over time.

Play Here, Go There

Just because you have chosen your home casino doesn't mean you can't visit and enjoy the others. Casinos have become big destination spots offering much more than just gambling and games. Fabulous restaurants, Broadway-style shows, and upscale shopping are just a few of the things available.

There is no reason that you shouldn't take advantage of all that the other casinos have to offer. Separate your playing time from other activities and plan your day accordingly. When it's time to play, do it in your core casino. Plan dinner breaks and other recreational time to enjoy what some of the other casinos have to offer.

The Royal Flush

Just about all of the high-end casinos in Las Vegas offer a free attraction many times a day. The volcano at the Mirage may be the most famous, but the fountain show at Bellagio is a must see.

If you do give into temptation and try a little action at another casino, make sure you sign up for their program so you can begin racking up those points.

Double the Fun

Once you do establish yourself at your home casino and build up some nice comps, then you can try venturing to a new place. Before you do, though, call ahead and let them know about your past play and that you are considering trying out their place. See what they can do for you.

Working the System

Comps are doled out not as a charitable gesture but because it makes good business sense on the part of the casino. Casinos enjoy a house edge on the games they offer so they want to keep their customers happy and coming back. The comps are there for the taking and there's certain things you can do to increase your share.

Never Leave Home Without It

First and foremost, if you are going to play, make sure you are getting credit. Whenever you leave the house, make sure you have your player's card with you. Before you pull a lever or push a button on a slot machine, make sure you swipe that card. If you are playing a table game, be sure to present your card before you place a bet.

On that rare occasion when you do leave your card home, you can easily get a replacement or temporary card. The only problem you may encounter, however, is a long line of savvy new players who know to get a card before they commence play. Don't let that deter you from getting that replacement card but let it serve as an incentive to never forget to bring your card with you.

> **Busted**
>
> When it comes to comps, don't get too greedy. If you are constantly asking for comps, complaining, or being unreasonable in your requests, you will soon develop a reputation as a comp pig and your business will become a lot less desirable.

Play Your Stakes

If you are a $25 per hand blackjack player, don't sit down to a $5 table and place your $25 bets. Casinos are very good at tracking your actual play, but why take that chance? Good floor people will know you are averaging $25 a bet even if you are at a lower denomination table but no one is perfect.

There always will be human error. You may get mistaken for the player next to you. A problem could arise at another table diverting the pit boss's attention. There could be everyday distractions keeping the casino workers from accurately recording your betting amounts. No one has as much at stake as you, so if you are going to play for $25 a hand, find a $25 minimum table so you get full credit.

Don't get too cute with your play, either. Some blackjack players will sit down to the $25 minimum tables and bet $25 a hand. Yet, when they sense the pit boss watching, they will increase their bets to $100 a hand in the hopes that the powers that be will think that they are betting that amount on a regular basis.

There are a few things wrong with this philosophy. Again, we can't state this enough, casinos are very good at tracking play and are unlikely to be fooled. Next, such wild fluctuations in betting amounts are indicative of card counting so you may be attracting the wrong kind of attention. Finally, you want to play your best. Comps are just secondary. So put your focus and attention on the game and let the comps take care of themselves.

Having said that, there is one trick you can employ that usually works well. Buy in for a large amount and start off with bigger than average bets. Then go back to your normal play after a short period of time. No one will accuse you of foul play and your comps will be bumped up a little.

No Need for Speed

While casinos have become much better at tracking play in this automated age, there is still a lot of guesswork. When you sit down to the table, you can be sure someone will have a fairly good idea of how much you are betting and how long you have played.

What isn't tracked is how many hands you have played or bets you have made. For instance, if you sit down to the blackjack table and play $25 a hand for four hours, then those numbers will be used in the formula that determines your theoretical loss (see Chapter 1) and will also be used to credit your account. How many hands you played in that four hours will not be calculated as long as you didn't leave the table for an extended period of time.

Why is this important? If the idea is to get the most bang for your buck, you are better off playing at a slow table than fast one. In blackjack, pick a table that has one open seat as opposed to an empty table. It takes a lot more time to deal to six players than one. If you are playing craps or roulette, gravitate toward the crowded tables. It will take a lot more time between rolls of the dice or spins of the wheel.

Some dealers may be slower than others. Spend enough time in a casino and you will figure them out. When the action is on you, you don't need to be in a hurry. There's no time clock for you to make a decision whether to stick or take a card in blackjack. Be thoughtful of the others playing with you, but take a couple of extra seconds. Over the course of time, those seconds will add up.

You can even work in bathroom breaks or cell phone calls away from the table while you sit out a few hands. You won't be penalized at all for taking a few short breaks. So, rather than sign out, take your breaks while you are playing.

Go for the Credit

The last thing you should ever do is play with money that is not designated as recreational funds. If you need the money for anything else, by all means don't gamble with it. So it should go without saying that you should never have a need for a line of credit with a casino. That's a short-sighted deal you shouldn't make, right?

If you are doing it on credit because you legitimately don't have the money to play, you shouldn't ask for credit. You should never gamble with money you don't have or can't repay. However, if you are gambling with credit for comps, then you should give it a go. When you sign up for your player's card, ask for a credit application to fill out as well. Assuming your credit history is in good standing, you should have no problem gaining access to free and easy credit.

This will establish your reputation with the casino as a serious gambler. Once the credit is in line, write a few *markers* to show that you are not afraid to use that credit line. Just make sure it's not for an amount you wouldn't have otherwise played for and pay off the markers soon after.

High Roller Talk

A **marker** is an IOU signed by a player to evidence an advance of credit from the casino. A marker is a real obligation just like any other debt you may incur. So use them as a matter of convenience not as a way to play when you can ill afford to do so.

Perception is often stronger than reality. With a credit line and a few placed markers, you should find yourself with better comps without having risked any more money.

Go When No One Else Does

Casinos operate 24 hours a day, 7 days a week. They never close their doors. Of course, some times are much busier than others. A summer weekend in Atlantic City will be overflowing with people compared to a mid-week January day.

A big convention or two can swell the overall numbers in Las Vegas. Every casino will be more crowded on long holiday weekends.

When casinos are busiest, they need your business the least. When they need your business the least, your rewards for playing won't be great. Even if you have comp dollars to spend, room rates will be higher during peak hours and restaurant reservations may be hard to come by. Even the buffet lines may be too long for your tastes.

If you have the flexibility, try to schedule your visits when the casinos are least crowded. It will be a lot easier to get a free room when the hotel is at 50 percent capacity than when it is overbooked. When pit managers aren't dealing with numerous crises, they are more likely to offer a food voucher. You are more likely to be able to use that food voucher when there is not a two-hour wait for every restaurant.

Bring a Friend or 10

There is power in numbers. If you have a group outing, use that to your advantage. Call various casinos ahead of time and let them know you have a large number of people looking to gamble and have a fun time. In return for the business, you want to know what they can promise up front.

You don't have to be exact but be honest with both the number of people and their level of play. If you have 8 people, half of which don't gamble at all, don't say you have 20 hard-core gamblers coming. Your credibility is on the line. If you do have 20 players ready for some action, try to secure tickets to a show or food vouchers ahead of time.

If everyone is staying the night, try for discounted rooms. At the very least, if you are taking them to your home casino, make sure you get some extra comps for yourself. Casinos want business and they should be very accommodating for a big group. Call around until you find one that suits your needs.

Don't Be Shy

Just as the squeaky wheel gets the oil, the extro-verted bettor gets the comps. Be polite, be courteous, and be friendly but don't be shy. While comps are earned primarily on your play, most casinos have some flexibility to offer some other comps.

Believe it or not, there are some players who don't want casinos knowing how much they play and they don't sign up for cards. That's one reason casinos must have the flexibility to offer comps outside what is earned and accounted for in their system. Don't expect free rooms but don't be afraid to ask for a meal voucher. What's the worst that can happen? A *pit boss* politely says no.

> **High Roller Talk**
>
> The **pit boss** is a casino employee assigned to a particular area to supervise dealers and keep a watchful eye on the tables in his immediate area or pit. The pit manager is in charge of enforcing casino policy for the table games and for making decisions whenever a problem or issue arises. The pit manager also has a customer service role and often can help with comps.

Everybody Knows Your Name

Introduce yourself to as many people as possible. Casinos are in the hospitality business so let them do their job. Take the time to shake hands with the dealer, pit boss, pit manager and any other official looking person you see. When in doubt, say hello.

You don't have to be a nuisance. A quick, friendly hello and introduction will go a long way. Soon, they will recognize you and be calling you by your first name. Human nature is consistent. Think about it, who would you rather comp for a free dinner? The person with a friendly smile who always says hi or the person whose first conversation with you is to ask for a freebie.

Every casino employee will have a nametag. Use them and address everyone by their first names. Be personable and you will be surprised at the positive reaction you will receive in return.

The Least You Need to Know

- Comps are earned over time, so try to give most of your play to one casino.
- Choose a casino that is a good match for your budget and level of play but make sure that casino has the amenities that appeal to you.
- Play at a table that offers minimum stakes that mirror your average bet.
- Be friendly and outgoing and treat every employee with respect—and when it's time, don't be shy about asking for comps.

Chapter **5**

Etiquette

In This Chapter

- Know the rules
- Your friend the dealer
- Play well with others
- Be realistic
- Tipping
- It's your birthday

Casinos have cameras, employees, and watchdogs everywhere. They have to keep an eye on everyone in order to maintain the integrity and security of the games. You can be fairly certain that if you are playing, someone is watching.

In many instances, there will be quite a few people observing you including dealers, pit bosses, and other players. Maintaining a high level of decorum and civility is not only courteous, but it's also good business sense. You don't want to be a jerk to the people rating you.

Handing out discretionary comps includes a human element. Comps are used to court valued customers. Someone who handles herself in a professional manner with a good understanding of what she's doing will be considered a valued customer.

Learn the Game

If you're going to play, learn not only the rules but the customs. It will make the game more enjoyable for you and those playing with you. We'll go over some of the customs here that may not be obvious but that a seasoned player should know. If you ever come across something that's not familiar to you, ask! Dealers are always happy to help.

Slot Etiquette

Playing a slot machine may seem fairly straightforward. After all, its only you and the machine. No other player or dealers to worry about. There are still, however, a few etiquette guidelines to follow.

- Slot machines are wildly popular and during busy times, they can quickly fill up. If the casino is busy (i.e, you notice that there are few machines available), don't play more than one machine at a time. If you want more action, play a higher denomination machine. Be respectful of the different types of machines available as well. Don't hog two *Wheel of Fortune* slot machines when those games are in demand.

- If you need to take a short restroom break, then either place a coin cup upside down over the lever of the machine, leave a coat on the chair, or lean the chair up against the machine. If you're going to take a break longer than a few minutes, then don't reserve a spot.

- If you're in a smoking area and want to smoke, use an ashtray. Be considerate of the person who comes next.

Table-Game Etiquette

Table games can be intimidating the first time playing. Unlike slot machines, you must be cognizant of the other players as well as the dealer. To make your time at the tables more enjoyable, here are a few etiquette guidelines to follow.

- When searching for a table, look for a placard, usually placed close to the dealer, that will state the minimum and maximum bets for that table.

- When buying in, wait for the current action to be completed and then place your cash on the table in front of you. Never hand cash directly to a dealer as she cannot take it from your hands. When the action stops, the dealer will take the money from the table and give you chips.

- In blackjack, if your cards are dealt face up, don't touch them. In any event, never remove cards from the table. When a new shoe is shuffled, you may be given the *cut card* to place anywhere in the deck.

> **High Roller Talk**
>
> A **cut card** is a solid plastic card used to cut the deck. If you're playing blackjack, the dealer may hand you a cut card once he's finished shuffling. Just place it anywhere in the middle of the cards.

- Never place a bet until all of the action from the previous bet is complete.

- When you leave the table, take your chips with you. You can only cash them at the cage, not at a table. You can, however, change up your chips (i.e., turn in five $5 chips for a $25 chip to make it easier to carry). You can always ask for a rack as well to carry your chips.

> **Jackpot**
>
> When you're the shooter in craps, make sure you throw the dice hard enough to hit the back wall of the table which is required to ensure a random roll.

Be Nice to Your Dealer

Dealers have a tough job and someone is always watching them. Casinos are one of the most highly regulated industries in the world. Dealers have very strict guidelines and rules that are in place to keep the game moving (so the casinos can make money) and to ensure the integrity and security of the game. For instance, in roulette, the dealer will start the ball spinning for a few moments before waving her hand and saying no more bets. Once she does that, don't place any more bets down.

Don't kill the messenger and don't blame the dealers for your losses. They have no control over whether you win or lose; they're just doing their jobs. Don't patronize them with comments that imply they are responsible for your success or failure. The dealer has no control over the randomness of the game. A player who blames them only shows his own ignorance. If you play enough, you'll witness your share of winning and losing streaks. Learn to take them in stride and keep them within your budget.

Don't question the authority of dealers. Put your bets down in time. If they say all bets are final, then that's that. Don't do anything to compromise their jobs.

If you believe they've made a mistake that affects you, politely point it out and explain the situation. Dealers aren't perfect and there will always be some human error. For instance, say you have 19 in blackjack and the dealer must stop at 18. He swipes your bet away by mistake even though you've won. Quickly, but politely, point out the mistake and, in this instance, put your hands on your cards to preserve them.

> **Busted**
>
> Never offer another player unsolicited advice. Everyone has their own quirks and unique playing styles. Even if their play is unorthodox, it's not your job to correct it, and the unsolicited advice may not be received very well, creating an uncomfortable environment for everyone. If you don't like how someone else is playing, you can always find another table.

Be Nice to Others

Casinos are open for you to enjoy, but they are not there for you alone. Tables can get very crowded so be respectful of others trying to play and make room. Seats at the blackjack and roulette table are for players only. If you have a companion with you, he'll have to stand.

Be respectful of other players when they are trying to make a decision. Give them the time you would expect. If they take too long, the dealer will hurry them up. If you intervene, you're only going to compromise the dealer's position and authority so leave it to him in the first place.

You never know who is watching you so don't draw unwanted attention to yourself. Nothing upsets dealers, pit bosses, and floor managers more than unruly customers. There's always a larger *crew* around the table then may be recognized. They look out for each other so be polite to all.

High Roller Talk _____

A number of dealers, called a **crew**, work the craps table.

Comps Are For Players

Casinos are happy to get your business, and they'll offer comps to get that business. Just remember that comps are earned. There is no entitlement to a comp. If you are not playing, don't ask.

When you do ask for comps, be realistic in your expectations. From our formula in Chapter 1, you should be able to estimate your worth to the casino. Keep your expectations in line and every-one will win.

When you are playing, remember that chips are real money. It's easy to forget when you are throw-ing chips around instead of cold, hard-earned cash. Those chips are worth just as much as the green stuff so don't get careless in playing for comps.

The Royal Flush

Many amateur blackjack players will get indignant and berate other players when they don't follow basic blackjack strategy. They get particularly angry over plays that cost them money conveniently forgetting the times that the bad play makes them money. The bottom line is that another player's decision has absolutely no bearing on your play at the blackjack table and seasoned players understand this.

It Takes Money to Make Money

Compiling comps is a way to make your gaming experience as cost effective as possible. So it would seem that tipping would be at odds with that goal. That would be dead wrong.

Dealers work very hard, and a good portion of their income is derived from tips. Tipping is an act of common courtesy and is expected. It's always easier to tip when you're winning but if you've played for a while, tip the dealer whether you win or lose. You can tip at any time, but whenever you or your dealer leave the table, it's a good idea to tip if you haven't already.

Tipping does not go unnoticed. We can't promise you that you'll get something extra in the way of comps every time you tip, but we can tell you that a poor tipper will rarely receive a discretionary comp.

Celebrate Another Year

When it comes to birthdays, let etiquette take a back seat. It's a time to celebrate you. Indulge, have fun, and take advantage of promotional giveaways. Many casinos offer gifts such as T-shirts, coffee mugs, dinner coupons, and matchplay dollars for showing up on your birthday.

 Jackpot

The Santa Fe Station Casino in Las Vegas offers a free $25 bet on the table game of your choice on your birthday—no strings attached. Just show up with valid identification and you get a free $25 bet even if you don't spend a dime.

Plan ahead and call around to see who offers what deals. Or check the websites of various casinos. You may be able to hit a number of casinos in a row and rake in a bag full of booty.

The Least You Need to Know

- You'll increase your chances of receiving comps if you look like you know what you're doing so learn the rules and etiquette of the games you play.

- You're constantly being observed so act professional and courteous at all times.

- Be respectful of the other players and avoid drawing unwanted attention to yourself.

- Remember to tip your dealers and you'll get a good reputation with the casino staff.

Chapter 6

Think Like a High Roller

In This Chapter

- Look the part
- Take comps with you when you travel
- Adopt the right attitude
- Live it up

If casinos relied only on high rollers, they wouldn't stay in business for very long. Fortunately, you don't have to be a high roller to be treated like one. Casinos aren't dummies. They have a pretty good idea what you're betting. There are things you can do to, however, to tip the scales in your favor. In this chapter, we look at what you can do to earn the high roller treatment.

Play the Role

If you want to be treated like a high roller, the first thing you'll have to do is look the part. Comps are given to attract repeat business. If you look like a homeless person, you're not likely to be wooed back. Rather, follow these guidelines.

- Dress nicely.
- Act cordial.
- Be polite.
- Exude confidence.
- Tip appropriately—if you don't have cash, use a *toke*.

 High Roller Talk _____

A **toke** is a tip given to dealers in the form of chips.

Give off an air of money and confidence and you greatly increase your credibility when you are asking for comps.

Have Comps, Will Travel

We learned earlier that the best way to rack up comps is to pick one favorite casino and do most, if not all, of your gaming there. That's still the rule of thumb, although like most rules, there are a few exceptions which are good to know.

Consolidation

The casino industry has undergone a huge wave of consolidation in recent years. Many properties now come under one corporate umbrella. The good news for players is that your player's card will often work seamlessly among all of the affiliated properties.

Companies like Harrah's have properties throughout the country. You can play slots at Harrah's racetrack casino in Chester, Pennsylvania one day and the points you earn are good at Harrah's Atlantic City the next. If you're traveling to a new city, find out if there is a sister casino you can visit.

Jackpot

With so much consolidation in the industry, many affiliated properties carry different names. For instance, Harrah's owns, among others, the Caesars, Showboat, Bally's, Horseshoe, Paris, and Rio casinos. If you go to the website of the casino you want to visit, you can usually find links to their sister properties as well.

One Card Deserves Another

Even if you are not going to an affiliated casino, all is not lost. Many casinos will honor your previous status. If you have a premium card at one casino, then you will usually be provided with a premium card at a new casino without having to earn your way up. Make sure you let the new casino know of your previous status.

Be a Winner

High rollers don't just blow into town, make one big bet and fly out again. At least, the valued high rollers don't. They are serious gamers. Even if you don't play at their limits, you can structure your play to improve your status. Appearances count and perception becomes reality. Here are some winner tips:

- **Play For Long Stretches.** Plan on playing when you have a good amount of time set aside. If you intend on playing for five hours that day, you are better off playing one five-hour session rather than breaking it up into three smaller sessions. You can still take some short breaks and you'll come across as a player who likes to play. For the same amount of action, you will look like a more serious player.

- **Show Your Stuff.** The casino floor is one of the few places in the world where it's acceptable to flaunt some money. Buy in for more than you intend to wager. Make the bets at the beginning and end of your sessions a little larger than normal.

  Never take chips off the table. If you are winning a good amount and want to book a win, resist the temptation to put them in your pocket. Have the discipline to keep them on the table for the whole world to see (especially the casino hosts). The fact that you have no intention of spending them is your little secret.

The Royal Flush

One of the most widespread legends of casinos is that they pump extra oxygen out to the casino floors to keep their patrons awake and gambling. Like most legends, this is false. Casinos give comps because the games are tilted in their favor. They don't need to resort to trickery.

- **Take Advantage.** During slow periods, there are usually incentives. Many casinos will have months where they offer promotions such as three times the cash back for your play. That means that you will earn comp dollars at three times the normal rate. So why not play during those times?

- **Move to the Front of the Line.** Some advantages can't be measured in absolute dollars. One of the biggest advantages a premium player's card offers is the ability to avoid waiting in line. Whether you are checking in or going to the buffet, there will often be a special line for premium card holders that will provide speedy service. In today's popular world, that can save you hours of time in just one visit. Your time is valuable.

In addition, there are some restaurants and private clubs reserved strictly for premium card members.

- **When in Doubt, Whip It Out.** Regardless of how much you play, just having a player's card can reap benefits. In addition to receiving promotional announcements, the card can be used at many retail and restaurant establishments on the casino property.

  You may not see any signs or advertisements, but whenever you make a purchase, ask if you can get a discount with your card. Whether you are getting a cup of coffee and a sandwich, buying a souvenir, or eating a nice meal for two, many places will offer a discount just for having the card.

 Jackpot

Take the time to ask a casino host or floor manager for a restaurant recommendation. Let it be known that you intend to eat your meals on the property. You may even want to ask for something that's good but quick because you want to get back to the games. Even if you don't get a comp, you're sending a message that you're spending your money on the property.

Living Large

A casino stay should be enjoyable. It's a recreational activity meant for pleasure and relaxation. As with your play, you should spend on amenities within your means. There are certain things you can do, however, to get the maximum value out of your nongaming spending.

Stay Where You Play

Casinos want all of your business. They want you to eat, breathe, sleep, and gamble in their establishments. You're more likely to receive favorable treatment if you are eating and sleeping on the premises rather than down the street. As a valued guest, you'll receive more promotional offers. In addition, casino hosts will take note of your spending habits.

If you are staying on the premises, there are more potential comps available. Casino hosts can offer upgraded rooms, free gym passes, spa treatments, or even treats such as afternoon teas or wine and cheese receptions available for hotel guests.

Busted

It's easy to get carried away with chips, casino credit, and room charges. Remember that it's the same as spending cash. Don't get carried away with your spending.

Charge It!

Charge everything you can to your room. This serves a couple of purposes. First, it will provide a good record of how much money you have spent at the casino, which can prove how valuable a customer you are. Next, it preserves potential comps.

For instance, say you go to the casino for a three-night stay. The first night after a few hours of gambling, you talk to a casino host about getting comped for dinner and he politely informs you that you haven't qualified. You go to dinner and charge it to your room. After three days, you have played quite a bit and now it's time to check out. Before you do, you talk to that casino host and share your hotel bill. That same dinner that wasn't comped before may be taken care of now that you have three day's worth of gaming in.

Cash Is Greener

Comp dollars are nice, but real dollars are better. Don't be shy about asking for cash back for your play. High rollers are routinely reimbursed their airfare and local transportation to visit a property.

Comp dollars have a value and cost the casino real money. Yes, they'd rather you spend that money back into the property. So if you don't ask, you won't get it. If you'd rather have cash than credit, ask a casino host what he can do for you. If you've really spent a lot of money, don't be shy about pulling out your airfare ticket and asking for reimbursement regardless of what you have in your comp dollar account.

The Least You Need to Know

- If you want to be treated like a high roller, dress the part.

- With so much consolidation in the casino industry, one card is good for all of the affiliated properties.

- If you have earned a premium card at one casino, any new casino you enter should offer you their premium card.

- All things being equal, stay and eat at your casino of choice.

- Don't be afraid to ask for cash instead of credits.

Chapter 7

Viva Las Vegas

In This Chapter

- A tale of two cities
- On the strip
- Downtown
- Off the strip
- Best places to play

Las Vegas is clearly the gaming capital of America, if not the world. Many a first-time visitor are amazed to walk off an airplane to hear the whir-ring of slot machines right there in the terminal. Unlike any other U.S. city, gambling permeates throughout the entire culture. Slot machines can be found in many unlikely places.

Las Vegas is also quite a tourist destination. In fact, Las Vegas has more hotel rooms than any other city in the United States with well over 130,000. With so many casinos and so many rooms, there is a lot of competition for your gambling dollar.

Which Las Vegas?

Las Vegas has many dimensions. There are upscale luxury resorts alongside of old Vegas-style gambling casinos. There's the decadence of the Strip and the quirkiness of Freemont Street. Then there are those casinos located just off the Strip.

We explore all of these in this chapter. In addition, there is a comprehensive casino guide located in Appendix B that highlights casinos in each of the geographic areas covered by this book.

The Royal Flush

The competition for your action continues to rise. In its most recently reported fiscal year, Las Vegas hotels and casinos on the Strip gave away over $1.3 billion worth of comps—an increase of 34 percent over the previous year.

A Season for Everyone

Las Vegas is the host city for many major conventions. That's why there are well over 130,000 hotel rooms. The good news for you is that there are plenty of times when Las Vegas is not playing host to so many people.

Sure, weekends are often crowded throughout the year, but there are many times when Vegas won't come close to capacity. Mid-summer and December are typically slow times. In addition, mid-week without a convention is slower than normal.

If you can be flexible, you can often find discounted, and even free, hotel rooms there for the taking. Shop around and ask for the cheapest rate. Don't be shy about speaking to a casino host to find if there are times when rooms can be had at a cut rate.

Busted

With so many conventions and tourist attractions, many nongamblers find themselves in Las Vegas on occasion. Because there is no avoiding the gambling culture, whether you are a gambler or a nongambler, be careful not to get caught up in the atmosphere and bet over your head.

The Center of It All

The Strip is that portion of Las Vegas Boulevard that hosts most of the premiere resorts in town and mainly stretches from Mandalay Bay in the south end to the Stratosphere to the north. Located in the heart of the Strip are the illustrious upscale properties of Caesars, Bellagio, Venetian, and Wynn.

The big resorts dwarf their smaller counterparts that are located sporadically throughout, such as the Barbary Coast. On a surface level look, one would think that the luscious resort properties cater to the big spenders, or *whales*. A check of their room rates would seem prohibitive. However, don't let that intimidate you.

High Roller Talk

A **whale** is an extremely high roller. You're sure to see a few at the upscale properties on the Strip.

If you are a slot or video poker player, there are bargains to be had. With plenty of machines to choose from at all price levels, you can earn comps in the lap of luxury. In addition, valued customers will receive good room offers. If you are a regular who enjoys the finer things in life, pick one of the nicer casinos for most of your play.

The upscale properties must compete for customers just like everyone else. The main difference between the luxury resorts and the smaller properties is how they compete. The top of the line resorts know that they will attract plenty of people who want to come in and see the free attractions and explore the property. So they don't need to offer free T-shirts or other promotional giveaways to get people in the door. Yet, they know if people stay there, they'll get most of their action.

The upside is that you will receive comps and room offers at some of the nicer resorts in the world. The rooms are luxurious and the restaurants are terrific. The other side of the equation is that you won't find a lot of cheap eats or promotions such as 99-cent shrimp cocktails. In addition, if you are a table-game player, playing games such as blackjack, craps, and roulette, you won't find any cheap table stakes. The minimum bets may take you out of your comfort zone.

Jackpot

At the cafe at Ellis Island casino, you can get a fabulous steak dinner including soup or salad, vegetable, and potato all for $4.95. It's available around the clock, but there's one catch. It's nowhere to be found on the menu. All you have to do is ask for it. Here's another tip. When you're done eating, ask for a $5 matchplay.

The smaller properties know that they won't get people in the door just to check them out. So that's where you will find many food bargains and promotional giveaways.

Take the time to explore the area and find favorite places to play and eat. A good option is to give one of the upscale resorts all of your slot play, but find some terrific meal deals at one of the smaller casinos that competes to attract customers. Some of these bargains are so good, that it's worth venturing out to another casino.

Glitter Gulch

Freemont Street is the center of downtown Las Vegas and represents old-style Vegas. Before the Strip was built up, *Glitter Gulch* was the center of gaming activities. Venerable properties such as Binion's Gambling Hall and Hotel, Four Queens, and the Golden Nugget are still there.

> **High Roller Talk**
>
> **Glitter Gulch** is the nickname for Freemont Street, located in the heart of downtown Las Vegas. It is so named because of all of the neon emanating from the old-time casino properties located there.

Downtown Las Vegas has a completely different look and feel from the Strip. The casinos are smaller and don't have the amenities that their upscale brethren on the Strip have, although the Golden Nugget was recently refurbished. Glitter Gulch caters to gamblers. They offer cheaper table stakes including single deck blackjack games at low minimums. If you enjoy your games without the frills, then Freemont Street is for you.

Glitter Gulch also has bargain food prices and cheaper rooms. From Binion's $1.99 breakfast to Golden Gate's 99-cent shrimp cocktail, the deals are plentiful. The room rates will be significantly less expensive than those on the Strip.

You'll also find things a little less formal downtown. If you are putting in the time playing, employees on the casino floor will have more discretion to offer you comps such as free rooms. Room availability is generally greater downtown as well because you are away from all of the major convention centers offering more opportunities for comps.

The Royal Flush

Las Vegas is known for its elaborate shows and its many free attractions such as the live pirate battle at Treasure Island. Perhaps the most fascinating of all is the Freemont Street Experience located over a pedestrian mall downtown. The Freemont Street Experience is an over-the-top light and laser show starting every hour on the hour from dusk to midnight.

Some Vegas Secrets

Away from the Strip and Glitter Gulch are some of the best-kept secrets in Las Vegas. There are a number of properties that offer great comp deals, cheap rooms, and bargain-priced buffets. These properties are often referred to as catering to "locals."

It's true you won't find dancing fountains and exploding volcano's, but it doesn't mean there aren't things to do besides gambling. Many of the properties have bowling alleys and movie theaters. With off-Strip prices, these properties are worth considering even if you're a visitor.

 Jackpot

At any one of the Station Casinos' properties—Boulder Station, Palace Station, Red Rock Resort, or Santa Fe Station—you receive free slot play just for signing up for a Boarding Pass slot club card. When you receive your card and set your pin, you just take the card to any slot or video poker machine and insert your card and pin. You will receive free slot play (as good as cash in the machine) anywhere from $5 to $500.

Sam's Town, Boulder Station, and Arizona Charlie's are three of the best off-Strip casinos. They each offer fantastic value when it comes to room, food, and comps!

Playing the Games

Not all games are created equal and Vegas has some interesting gaming laws that you need to know about. Here's a rundown of some of the more popular games.

- Roulette tables can have a single zero or double zero. The single-zero tables have a 2.7 percent house edge while the double-zero tables have a 5.26 percent house edge. Many casinos on the Strip offer single-zero tables but the minimums are high. Some downtown casinos offer single-zero tables and have smaller minimums, but make sure you are at a single-zero table before sitting down.

- The casinos on Glitter Gulch offer the best single-deck blackjack games. In Vegas, some tables only pay 6-5 for blackjack as opposed to 3-2. This change dramatically ups the house edge so make sure you find a table paying 3-2.

- The Nevada Gaming Control Board publicizes slot payback percentages annually by area. For the most recent period (ending June 30, 2006), downtown off-Strip casinos offered better returns for customers than machines located on the Strip.

The Least You Need to Know

- With an abundance of hotel rooms, deals can be had in Las Vegas during slow periods such as December.

- Even the upscale resorts will offer their valued customers good room deals.

- The best food deals and promotional giveaways will be found at the smaller properties.

- There is plenty of free entertainment throughout Las Vegas.
- Look downtown on Freemont Street for cheaper rooms and great food deals.

Chapter 8

Down the Shore

In This Chapter

- The next Vegas
- A gambler's world
- On the boardwalk
- The Marina district
- A look at the games

Atlantic City was a city on decline when gambling was legalized in 1976. The first casino doors opened to large crowds in 1978, but it did little to improve the plight of the surrounding city. The casinos were often considered a respite in an otherwise depressed atmosphere.

If you haven't been to Atlantic City recently, things have changed dramatically. With the opening of the Borgata Hotel and Casino in 2003, the ante was upped throughout this ocean town. The Borgata represents the first truly upscale resort, offering first-class amenities, and became a worldwide destination.

The rest of Atlantic City quickly took note. The other casinos feverishly tried to keep pace by remodeling or building new towers. Those casinos on the boardwalk opened beach bars and other attractions to lure in customers. New world-class restaurants are popping up at every casino as each tries to one-up the other.

Outside of the casinos, much is changing as well. From the convention center as you enter off the Atlantic City expressway to the Walk, a pedestrian mall filled with outlet shopping, Atlantic City is truly turning a corner. It's not quite Vegas, but it's getting there.

Come to Play

Traditionally, Atlantic City has never been the entertainment destination that Las Vegas is. Atlantic City has appealed to gamblers and that's where the casinos made all of their money. It's important to note because the comp system reflects that culture.

Hotels and casinos weren't trying to attract families or tourists to spend money in their hotels, restaurants, and shows. They wanted to attract gamblers who wanted action.

Day Trippin'

Being located a couple hours drive south of New York City and just an hour east of Philadelphia, Atlantic City has long appealed to day trippers.

Go to any casino mid-morning and you'll see a steady stream of busses shipping gamblers in for the day.

People will depart the bus, receive a coupon for a free roll of quarters or some other promotional giveaway, and head right to the line to get their prize. Players literally receive their first comp before they even place a bet. Players who want to travel to other casinos can easily take a *jitney* around town.

High Roller Talk

A **jitney** is a small bus that cruises around Atlantic City 24 hours a day. It's only $2, it will take you near any casino, and you'll rarely have to wait more than a few minutes for the next one to appear.

No Room at the Inn

Atlantic City has only about 15,000 hotel rooms which is just a tiny fraction of the 130,000 plus that Las Vegas houses. That changes the dynamic of comps dramatically. If you are a heavy or regular player, you can still count on getting free rooms. You're going to be first in line.

For the rest of us, though, we'll have to work a little harder. If you sign up for a player's card, you'll find yourself receiving plenty of offers in the mail. They may not be for free rooms, but you'll receive discounts or package deals including dinner, spa treatments, or even coupons to spend in any restaurant or store of your choice.

As Atlantic City is changing, so are the comps and promotions. Caesars, for instance, offers room packages that include $50 for you to spend at any of the fine shops or restaurants located at the prestigious Pier at Caesars.

> **Busted**
>
> Don't take a last-minute trip to Atlantic City and expect to find a hotel room. With a shortage of rooms, you need to book far ahead of time in order to ensure a room and a reasonable rate.

Your Presence Is Required

Most of the casinos in Atlantic City offer similar promotions in addition to the regular comps based on play. All of these promotions are aimed at getting you in the door and having you sign up for a card.

First, just by having a card, you are eligible for the many daily giveaways typically offered. The only requirements are that you show up and either swipe your card on a slot machine once or check to see if you won.

Next, your player's card is usually good for a substantial discount at many restaurants or shops on the property. With so many more fine choices, this can be a real benefit.

The Royal Flush

There's a common misconception that casinos want you to sign up for their cards so they can track your play and report you to the IRS. Yes, they'll track your play but that's a good thing. They want your name and address primarily so they can send you promotions, reward you with comps, and attract your business. There are strict guidelines about what needs to be reported to the IRS and whether you have a card or not will have no bearing on that reporting obligation.

Finally, most of the properties offer double points during certain weeks or months. With so few casinos in Atlantic City, the comp structure and promotions are similar throughout the city.

Jackpot

Self-parking lots in Atlantic City casinos charge a flat fee of $4–$5 for a 24-hour period. Take your receipt with you and you can park in one other casino lot for free during that 24 hour period. Better yet, take advantage of valet parking which doesn't cost any more and allows you to pull right up to the front door.

The bottom line is that you should pick a primary casino to call home and give most of your action to. Pick the one that has the amenities and location that you desire, take advantage of their promotions, and do all of the things discussed in the previous chapters.

On the Beach

From the Hilton in the south to the Showboat in the north, casinos dot the length of the boardwalk. Stay at any property on the boardwalk and you can explore the others during a leisurely stroll along the boardwalk. If the walk is too much, there are ample rolling chairs that seat two. Expect to pay about $1 a block.

Because many of the promotions in Atlantic City require your presence, hitting one of the boardwalk properties is a good idea. You can play primarily at one but still enter the giveaways at the others. Caesars is right in the middle and has the world-class Pier at Caesars.

Atlantic City airport is only 14 miles outside of the city but flights can be expensive. A cheaper alternative is to fly into Philadelphia and take a train from Philly to Atlantic City.

Off the Boardwalk

In the Marina district are Harrah's, Trump Marina, and the Borgata. The benefit of Harrah's and Trump Marina are that they are both located right on the water and each include a great number of boat slips. It's not convenient, however, to walk from property to property in the Marina district.

Harrah's has undergone extensive renovations and in the summer of 2007 opened what it calls The Pool. The Pool is the largest swimming pool in the city and is just part of the continuing transformation of Atlantic City from gambling destination to resort city.

The Borgata is the undisputed crown jewel of Atlantic City. It's a world-class operation with outstanding amenities. The comp system and promotions are as good as any other casino. The only downside is that the casino is so popular that getting a room or into a restaurant can be difficult on weekends.

 Jackpot

At the Trump Taj Mahal, there's a well-kept secret above the poker room. The Taj has one of the biggest—and most crowded—poker rooms in Atlantic City. If you find yourself hungry but don't want to be away from your table for too long, ask for the poker snack room. There are no signs for it: it's up one floor above the poker room, and you have to take a hidden elevator up to it. The snack bar itself is not real scenic, but it offers quick, good inexpensive meals. If you've been playing for a while, ask the floor manager for a comp.

The Games Played

For the most part, the gaming is fairly standard in Atlantic City. You won't find much difference in games from casino to casino. The one thing you will find is that the minimum bets on table games are fairly high especially at nights and on weekends. Unlike Las Vegas, where there are so many casinos offering games at all wage levels, Atlantic City doesn't have that diversity. So, if you are a low-stakes table-game player, be aware that it may be hard to find a table to your liking. In addition, at peak times, it may be hard to find a slot or video machine to your liking.

Roulette in Atlantic City is different from Las Vegas. Most tables use double-zero wheels, but the casino is only allowed to take half of your wager on even money bets (such as red/black or odd/even) when zero or double zero come up. This lowers the even money bets to 2.63 percent. However, the edge on all other bets remains at a high 5.26 percent.

The Royal Flush

Contrary to some beliefs, slot machines are never due—even if they haven't paid out in a while. The machines are equipped with a random number generator to pay out a certain percentage so that each new spin stands the same chance as the one before.

The Least You Need to Know

- Atlantic City has a shortage of hotel rooms which makes room offers a tougher opportunity than in Las Vegas.

- Because Atlantic City attracts a lot of gamblers down for the day, many of the casinos' promotions are geared toward attracting you onto their gaming floors.

- The opening of the upscale Borgata has spurred a whole new wave of development in Atlantic City with many of the casinos building new hotel towers and adding upscale restaurants and shops.

Chapter **9**

On the Reservation

In This Chapter

- A recent phenomenon
- Similar to Vegas
- Similar to Atlantic City
- A look around the nation

From humble origins, Native American reservation casinos have exploded across the American landscape. From coast to coast, there are now over 360 casinos ranging in various sizes in 30 different states. This chapter looks at how you can get the most comps for your buck at a reservation casino.

A Little History

In order to understand the nature of Native American casinos and the types of comps that they are likely to offer, it helps to know a little bit of the background.

The history of gambling on Native American reservations originated in the 1970s with a tribe in Florida that offered high-stakes bingo. The popularity of this game ignited a firestorm of controversy throughout the courts.

The various court cases spurred Congress to take action and in 1988, it passed the landmark *Indian Gaming Regulatory Act*, which allows Native American Reservations to host gambling centers on their land so long as the state in which the reservation is located has some sort of legalized gambling.

> **High Roller Talk**
>
> IGRA is an acronym for the **Indian Gaming Regulatory Act,** the legislation that authorizes Native American casinos.

Because most states have some sort of legalized gambling, the result has been nothing short of changing the entire landscape of casino gambling in the United States. No longer limited to a few select locales, Native American casinos broke down barriers and have helped ignite further casino development outside of reservations.

> **The Royal Flush**
>
> When congress passed IGRA, it was hard to imagine how quickly and far Native American casinos would grow. Many congressmen thought they were authorizing quaint local bingo parlors, not the behemoth casinos that would follow.

A Continuing Evolution

Native American casinos have advanced far from their bingo origins. Today, these casinos spread throughout the land, and bring in more gaming revenue than Las Vegas and Atlantic City combined—close to $20 billion a year.

It is a huge industry and as you can expect with an industry that big, many players are involved. Big corporate conglomerates such as Harrah's, MGM Grand, and Hard Rock have partnered with some of the Native American reservations. In addition, some of the larger Native American casinos, such as Foxwoods and Mohegan Sun, are branching out of the reservations. Both Foxwoods and Mohegan Sun are partners in Pennsylvania casinos that are not being built on reservations.

What that means for you is that there is plenty of consolidation in this market. Do your research and find out what casinos have affiliations with others. This will allow you to transport your comps from casino to casino.

In addition, the larger Native American casinos are just like the majority of casinos throughout this country. The rules and tips contained in this book will be just as applicable.

 Jackpot

On Foxwoods website, www.foxwoods.com, you can sign up to receive promotional offers even if you've never played there before.

A Little Bit of Vegas

Many of the Native American casinos bear little resemblance to the bingo parlors of the '70s that preceded the passing of the IGRA. These are full-scale casinos with all of the bells and whistles of their Las Vegas brethren.

Hotel and casino properties, such as Foxwoods and Mohegan Sun in Connecticut and the Seminole Hard Rock properties in Florida, are huge destination resorts that offer everything a gaming enthusiast needs under one roof. When it comes to gaming, restaurants, shopping, and first-class accommodations and amenities, Las Vegas has nothing on these properties.

The Royal Flush

Foxwoods Casino, located in Mashantucket, Connecticut, is the largest casino in the United States and is owned by the Mashantucket Pequot Tribe.

A Little Bit of Atlantic City

When it comes to comps, Las Vegas still has the best food and room deals. With so much competition centered in one area, Las Vegas has to appeal to the most basic comp needs. If you recall, Atlantic City's basic comp system centers around promotional activities to get you in the door and on the gaming floor, if not necessarily to stay on the property.

Expect more Atlantic City–type comps when it comes to Native American casinos. If you're a regular gamer, you'll earn your room comps. But for the casual player, look more for discounts and take advantage of daily promotions. You won't find 99-cent shrimp cocktail specials, either. However, if you've played for a while, ask for food comps.

Busted

In many jurisdictions, there is no public information available concerning the payback percentages of gaming machines located in Native American casinos. This doesn't mean that the machines aren't regulated, but the customer won't be able to pick a casino with a higher payback percentage.

From Coast to Coast

As you would expect, Native American reservations are located throughout the United States from coast to coast. Casinos have jumped up from urban areas to more secluded areas. In fact, some of the fastest growing venues are in rural Oklahoma and California.

This changing landscape not only affects local markets but the national market as well. With so many choices, the competition for your business only increases. More and more comp dollars are being spent to attract customers in the industry overall.

Every casino is aware of this and sensitive to this fact. Just because a casino doesn't have a lot of direct local competition doesn't mean it won't be offering comps.

 Jackpot

Oklahoma is home to a great number of Native American casinos and proves that even in a rural setting, casinos can offer a first-rate experience. The Choctaw Casinos have eight properties in Oklahoma and offer great promotional offers.

From State to State

Native American casinos will vary greatly from state to state. Some states such as Connecticut allow full service casinos with the whole gamut of games. Others offer more limited gaming. The legal payout amounts on slot machines will differ as well.

Under the IGRA, Native American casinos are allowed gaming in three different classes. Class I allows minimum games that would be more suited to a church carnival than a casino. Class II offers bingo and related games along with games that are played against other players (and not the house) such as poker.

Finally, Class III casinos offer the full suite of games. Reservations may operate as Class III casinos only if the state they're located in authorizes such games and the reservation enters into a deal with the state.

If you're scheduling a trip, be sure to ascertain what types of games will be offered so you won't be disappointed.

Size Matters

The closer an Indian casino is located to a big city, typically the bigger the casino will be. Connecticut's Foxwoods and Mohegan Sun, located not far from New York and Boston, are behemoths with all the amenities and the ability to offer first-class comps, such as free rooms, meals at upscale restaurants, and reimbursed travel if your play warrants it.

Foxwoods is one of the largest hotel and casinos in the world and offers something for everyone. There are three major hotels on site with various price points. Lake of Isles golf courses are close by and Foxwoods offers room/golf packages to play at these top notch courses. The Spa at Foxwoods offers a first class and full array of services.

With over 7,000 slot and video poker machines, Foxwoods has plenty of promotions for the low level gambler. There are daily giveaways for swiping your "Wampum Rewards Card." The first day you get your card, Foxwoods will pay back 120% of your slot machine losses in the form of bonus slot pay up to a maximum of $250.

Some of the more remote and smaller casinos will have a harder time offering competitive comps especially if they have limited game offerings. In addition, the restaurant choices on site may be severely limited, often not much more than one coffee shop or a few kiosks.

The Royal Flush

Many tribes own more than one casino. The 360-plus Indian Reservation casinos are owned by approximately only 225 federally recognized tribes.

The Least You Need to Know

- There are over 360 Indian Reservation casinos spread throughout the United States.
- Indian Reservation casinos generate more money than those casinos in Las Vegas and Atlantic City combined.
- Some of the biggest ones offer top of the line amenities and world-class restaurants.

- Indian Reservation casinos are similar to Atlantic City in that they offer promotions that require your presence while room offers are harder to come by.

- The lines have blurred between Native American reservations and other casinos. Big corporations such as Harrah's and Hard Rock have part ownership in Native American casinos so call to see if your comps can travel with you.

Chapter 10

Casino Nation

In This Chapter

- A look around the country
- Down in the delta
- At the racetrack
- On a riverboat

No longer confined to Nevada and New Jersey, there are casinos in 37 states. From riverboats to racetracks, they come in every shape and size. From California's famed card rooms to slots-only casinos, they all have one thing in common—they want your business and they'll offer comps to get it.

Not All Casinos Are Created Equal

There is now some form of casino in the great majority of states. From urban centers such as Detroit to rural outposts in New Mexico, casinos are thriving and the trend is that more are better. With the baby boomers starting to ease into retirement, you can expect more competition for entertainment dollars including gambling.

The Royal Flush

There's a common misconception that table-game players are treated better than slot players. Slot players are extremely valued and welcomed. Slot machines don't take up a lot of space, don't cost as much money to operate, and offer a larger casino edge. So you can trust that casinos want the slot player's business.

Every state has its own quirks and rules so before embarking on any trip, check to see what games are available. Betting limits may vary greatly as well. Each state also has different ways of reporting the payback percentages of casinos located in its jurisdiction.

All of the tips and guidelines learned in the previous chapters generally hold true for just about any casino. As a step-by-step look at every casino is well beyond the scope of this book, here are some universal hints to keep in mind:

- Casinos in geographic areas with lots of competition are more competitive with their comps.
- Expect Atlantic City–type comps in most locales.
- Be polite and thankful for any comps you receive and manage your expectations, especially in smaller, more remote locations.

- The growing number of casinos all over the country is creating a national market so just about every casino realizes it doesn't have a captive audience and it must compete with comps.

 Jackpot

Beau Rivage Resort and Casino offers complete vacation package deals that are all-inclusive of air and ground transportation, room, and food. See their website www.beaurivageresort. com for details.

Along the Mississippi

The state of Mississippi has become home to a large number of casinos. They are primarily broken down into two areas: Tunica and Biloxi. While technically, the casinos are supposed to be riverboats, they are real buildings built on barges that stay docked 24 hours a day.

While not quite Vegas, Tunica rivals Atlantic City in number of casinos and quality of gaming alternatives. It is a full-fledged casino town. With not nearly the daily visitors of Atlantic City, Tunica is one of the few spots outside of Vegas where there are plenty of hotel room choices. With warmer weather and more reasonable rates, Tunica is an affordable alternative to Atlantic City.

Busted

On all jackpots paying $1,200 or more in a Mississippi casino, the casino is required to withhold 3 percent of your winnings and make a nonrefundable payment to the Mississippi Tax Commission as a gambling tax.

Biloxi is, or was, a casino town much like Tunica or Atlantic City. Located on the Gulf of Mexico, this town was devastated by Hurricane Katrina. The good news is that most of the casinos have been rebuilt (or are in the process of being rebuilt) and Biloxi is open for business. With plenty of rooms, lots of gaming, and the Gulf Coast at your doorstep, Biloxi can be a real gaming destination.

Many of the big corporate names have properties located in both Tunica and Biloxi. For those who like to travel, you can try the Mississippi casinos and still earn comps that you can take with you. In addition, call ahead of time and let them know your betting history to see if you qualify for free room and drink.

A Day at the Races

Racinos are a natural marriage of two venerable gambling institutions—racetracks and casinos. This has become a fairly popular way for states to introduce casino-style gambling without raising alarm among anti-gambling voters. The logic behind it is that gambling is already permitted at the racetrack so what's the harm in adding a few slot machines.

Racinos differ from state to state in the states that allow them. Often, there is not a hotel connected to the racino. However, the casino is usually open longer than the track whether it's racing season or not. Some are open 24 hours a day while others have limited hours. Be sure to check ahead as to how long the casino is open.

Also be sure to check out what types of games are offered. Many racinos offer only slot machines and other electronic gaming devices. These machines have become quite sophisticated, however. Games such as blackjack and keno can be offered. Still, other racinos may offer low-stakes table games such as poker.

Busted

Poker is one of the fastest-growing games in casinos. Once an afterthought, many casinos are either building or expanding their poker rooms and offering daily poker tournaments. Casinos want poker players but don't expect much in the way of comps. Poker is played against other players and the casinos only make money by taking a small cut of each pot. Depending on the stakes you are playing, expect to earn only about 50 cents to $2 in comps for every hour played.

Down the River

The state of Iowa was the first state to legalize riverboat gambling and appropriately enough the first gaming ships set sail on April Fools Day, 1991. The reason that day is appropriate is that today just about any riverboat is anything but a boat.

The great majority are real buildings built on barges that don't move anywhere. In fact, in the aftermath of Hurricane Katrina, the Mississippi legislature took a common-sense approach and authorized casinos to build on land within so many feet of the shoreline.

About the only place you'll still find gambling boats is along the Atlantic coast. Ships set sail, taking off from the shore in Florida, Georgia, and South Carolina. These are real boats, and they must move to get out far enough off the coast to allow for the casino to open. Each ship will have different game offerings.

The real lesson to be learned from riverboat gaming is that casinos are here to stay. Gambling on riverboats was originally passed to allow for ships to float down the Mississippi as a leisurely activity. Much like racinos, it was a compromise legislation to generate tax revenue through gambling. Once established, the lines were muddied with barges and now building along the shoreline.

You can bet on the fact that casinos are expanding in the United States, and that's good news for you. The more properties, the more competition for your action.

What's Ahead?

There are many changes being implemented in the casino industry that will allow casinos to offer more personalized service. As things become more automated, the comp system will be more efficient.

An Automated World

Slot machines can already track individual play. In the future, slot machines will be programmed from a central site meaning that every machine will be a portal for different games. No longer will there be a wait for the more popular machines.

Walk up to a slot machine, swipe your card, and you will get a message asking if you wish to play your favorite game. You will be able to track and redeem comps right on the machine. Personal advertisements and promotions may appear that will appeal to you. This automation will lead to a merger of hospitality and slots.

We're just starting to see the beginning of casino chips imbedded with radio frequency identification chips or RFID. RFID chips will prevent counterfeiting but they can also be used to track play at table games. While widespread rollout is still a few years away, once implemented, you can rest assured that you will receive full credit for your play.

Increased automation already provides real time tracking of your play. This is great for players as casinos continue to consolidate. The MGM Mirage family of casinos offers this. If you're staying at

MGM Grand and want to play at Mirage no problem. You can play at Mirage in the morning, walk back to MGM Grand to check out and ask for a discount based on that morning's play.

> **Jackpot**
>
> Don't be shy about sharing personal information. Casinos use their databases to offer little perks and rewards. For instance, if a casino knows that your favorite drink is white wine, a bottle may be waiting in your room upon check-in.

More Consolidation

With increased consolidation in the casino industry, players paradoxically will have more choices. No longer will they be resigned to putting all of their chips in one casino basket. They can play at any number of family casinos across the country and their comps are good at all of them.

The increased consolidation won't limit choices just to high rollers, either. Every casino will want players but some systems will appeal to different clientele. The MGM Mirage group appeals to a more upscale crowd than Harrah's properties. But even within each family, there are casinos with varying amenities and hotel prices.

The Least You Need to Know

- Casinos in geographic areas with plenty of competition will be more aggressive with comps and promotions.

- Every state has different gaming laws, so call casinos in advance to see what games and limits are available.

- Tunica and Biloxi, Mississippi have close to the number of casinos as Atlantic City with more affordable hotel room rates.

- The tips and guidelines learned in this book are generally true no matter where you go.

Chapter 11

Around the World

In This Chapter

- Treading international waters
- A look up north
- In the Caribbean
- Across the pond
- The new casino capital of the world
- Online casinos

When it comes to casinos, the United States doesn't have anything on the rest of the world. The industry is thriving around the globe. The currency and language may change and some games may be different, but one thing remains constant; casinos want your business and will reward you for your play. While there may be some nuances in each market, the tips outlined previously in this book will serve you well.

Out to Sea

In the last chapter, you saw that riverboat casinos are a bit of a misnomer. The majority of these casinos are built on barges and for all practical purposes are really no different than land-based casino properties.

The one place, however, where you'll still find gambling boats is along the Atlantic coast. Ships set sail, taking off from the shore in Florida, Georgia, and South Carolina. These are real boats and they must move to get out far enough off the coast to allow for the casino to open. Each ship will have different game offerings.

 Jackpot

No matter where you play, rule number one when it comes to comps is if you don't ask, you don't get. Don't be shy about asking for rewards.

These true riverboat casinos are fairly low-budget affairs and cater to tourists and casual players. Many will offer coupons and discounts, and if you're bringing a big group, call ahead and see if you can get a group discount.

North of the Border

The gaming landscape in Canada is similar to that in the United States. There are over 100 casinos in Canada spread from coast to coast. The types of casinos range from the full-scale hotel resort casinos to the racinos where slot machines can be found at race tracks. The games offered at the full-scale casinos will be similar to those offered in the United States. Payouts and comp calculations will be the same as well.

Unlike the United States, there is not a central hub such as Atlantic City or Las Vegas. Ontario, Canada has the most casinos and gambling establishments of all the provinces in Canada. Niagara Falls and Woodstock are two cities in Ontario with a number of full-scale casinos. You'll find more competition for your dollars where there are more casinos.

The Royal Flush

Texas hold 'em poker, the quintessential American game, is quickly gaining worldwide popularity and games can be found at casinos around the globe.

Casinos in Paradise

Throughout the Atlantic and Caribbean are island destinations with a growing casino economy. These casinos cater to American tourists with many offering sports-book wagers that can be made on all the popular American sports.

The Atlantis resort on Paradise Island, Bahamas is a luxurious resort with a full-scale casino. They offer generous comps and the amenities are first rate. Because of the expense of travel required for most of its visitors to reach the Atlantis, most of their comps are geared to the mid- to high-level gambler. In order to entice gamblers back, the Atlantis offers periodic invitation only slot and blackjack tournaments with large prizes.

In addition, rooms are used to lure the desired gambler back. Even if its your first time visiting Atlantis, call ahead and let them know your history and where you play. A phone call or two on their part and you may well be comped before you arrive.

One unique feature of Atlantis is that you have your choice of signing up for a player's card or using your room key at the tables or slots. Either way, you can accumulate points.

Luxury casinos are prevalent throughout the Caribbean. There are well over 100 casinos throughout the various islands. Netherlands Antilles, Aruba, Antigua, the Dominican Republic, and Jamaica each boast a number of full scale casinos attracting tourists from North America and Europe.

A Look at Europe

Casinos can be found throughout Europe. Once a staple of Western European countries, gaming is a fast-growing industry in Eastern Europe as well.

For the most part, the types of games offered are similar to American-style casinos.

There are, however, a few differences between the casinos. Some casinos in Europe will require a membership, which usually involves a nominal fee. Smoking will be more prevalent than in the United States. In addition, the dress requirements may be different. Even if there is not a formal dress requirement, dress to fit in.

You will greatly increase your chances of receiving comps if you do your best to fit in. Here are a few pointers to keep in mind:

- Dress nicer than the average clientele in the casino.

- Learn to speak a few words of the native language. At the very least be able to say "hello" and "thank you" in the foreign language. When asking for comps, make every attempt to speak in the host's language.

- Be extremely courteous to all of the casino workers and inquire as to appropriate tipping amounts.

- Keep track of your play in both American dollars and the foreign currency. You want to keep track in American dollars so you don't play over your head. You will want to keep track in the foreign currency, so you know how many comps you have earned.

Jackpot

No matter where you play, call ahead and ask to speak with a casino host. Even if the casino is in another country, often they can offer comps based on your play at home.

An Exploding Market

Far East Asia represents the world's fastest growing casino market. Casinos are located in Taiwan, North and South Korea, Mongolia, China, and Vietnam. In China, the only place where legalized gambling is allowed is in Macau.

Macau is quickly becoming the gaming capital of the world. World-class casino hotel and resorts have opened and more are on the way. Many of the U.S. conglomerates are building properties there so western travelers will see a recognizable brand and can take comfort knowing that their comps will travel.

Should I Or Shouldn't I?

The explosion of online gaming in recent years has been severely tempered with the passage of the UIGEA. While many online sites will no longer serve U.S. customers, online gaming is not going away. Perfectly legal in most of the world, there are still a few secure sites that allow U.S. customers to play.

Busted

The Unlawful Internet Gambling and Enforcement Act or UIGEA was a law passed surreptitiously by the United States Congress as an addition to the Safe Ports Act in September 2006. The UIGEA did not make it illegal to gamble online per se, but it prohibits banks or financial institutions from processing transactions for online gaming operations.

With the uncertainty of the legal status in the United States, there are inherent risks in playing online. If you reside outside the United States, though, there are plenty of comps that can be earned from the comfort of your own home. Many sites offer deposit bonuses.

For example, a site may offer a 25 percent deposit bonus. So, if you deposit $100 and meet the minimum amount of play required, you will receive $25 whether you won or lost. Typically, you will track points with your play that can be redeemed for gifts. Other rewards programs include refer a friend, where both you and your friend can receive bonuses based on your friend signing up and playing.

Before you play, you should research the laws of your jurisdiction and decide for yourself if it's okay to play.

A Few Final Words

If you enjoy recreational gaming, then hopefully you've learned a few tips throughout this book that will help make your experience more enjoyable and more profitable. Be knowledgeable and confident.

Learn Video Poker

Because slot machines are the leading form of gambling, chances are that many readers will be primarily slot players. If you are a slot machine junkie, do yourself a favor and learn video poker. There are plenty of good books on the subject and it's an easy game to understand. If you know what you're doing, you're expected rate of return on video poker is substantially higher than on other slot machines. You'll be able to play a lot longer on the same bankroll and increase your comp earnings. For additional resources, please see Appendix C.

Play with Your Head

It's worth repeating. Play within your means and not over it. Never play for comps. Play because you enjoy it and its entertainment for you. The idea behind this book is to help you get the most comp benefit out of your normal play, not to increase your play or put you in a position of risking more than you can afford to lose.

No matter the game you are playing, you will have winning and losing streaks. When you are running good, save money for a rainy day. When you are running *cold*, stay within your budget.

High Roller Talk

A player on a losing streak or a slot machine that doesn't pay out is referred to as **cold**.

The Least You Need to Know

- No matter where you play, the same general guidelines learned throughout this book should apply.

- Learn the local mores and customs such as dress and tipping.

- Keep track of your play in the foreign currency so you know how many comps you're earning.

- Online sites offer rewards programs but there are inherent risks for U.S. players.

Glossary of Terms

Please note that not all of these terms are used in this book. However, they are all terms that you are likely to hear bantered about in a casino so they are included here for your reference.

action: Generally, placing any wager. Specifically, the amount of money a player wages during the course of a playing session.

anchor: The player sitting in the last position before the dealer at a blackjack table. This is the person who makes the final decision, thereby anchoring the game.

ante: A term used in certain poker games to refer to the amount that each player is required to put into the pot before a new hand can begin.

any craps: A one-roll dice bet in craps covering the 2, 3, or 12.

any seven: A one-roll dice bet in craps covering any 7.

baccarat: A card game played in casinos in which two or more players gamble against the banker. The player who holds two or three cards that total closest to 9 wins.

bankroll: The total amount of money a player has set aside for gaming. It's a good idea to keep this account separate from any funds needed for other purposes.

basic blackjack strategy: The mathematically correct way to play blackjack in order to maximize your advantage.

bet: A wager or gamble.

betting limits: The minimum and maximum that can be wagered on one bet as set by the casino.

betting right: In craps, betting on the Pass Line or with the shooter.

betting wrong: In craps, betting on the Don't Pass Line or against the shooter.

blackjack: A card game where the players try to beat the dealer by getting closest to 21 without going over. Also known as 21.

blackjack hand: A hand whose first two cards total 21 such as an Ace and a Ten. In blackjack, an Ace can count as 1 or 11.

blind bet: In Texas Hold 'Em poker, a bet that certain players are required to make before the cards are dealt as a result of their betting position. The position changes with each deal so that the players will take turns posting a blind bet.

bluff: A poker term used to describe a player making a bet with an inferior hand hoping to induce another player with a stronger hand to fold.

box: In craps, the area of the dice table controlled by the boxman where the center bets are placed.

boxcars: In craps, when you roll two sixes.

boxman: The casino dealer in charge of the craps table.

bump: To raise the previous bet in poker.

bust: To exceed 21 in blackjack, which automatically makes the hand a losing one.

casino hosts: Employees who are at the casino to look out for the needs of the casino's customers. They are there to help with everything in connection with a guest's relationship with the casino.

card counting: A system in blackjack to keep track of the percentage of high to low cards remaining in the shoe. Implemented correctly, a player can reduce the house advantage.

Caribbean stud poker: A five-card poker game where all players play against the house.

check: In poker, a term to describe a player's option to pass rather than bet so long as no one has bet in front of her.

chips: Tokens of varying denominations used at gaming tables in lieu of cash.

cold: A term referring to a player on a losing streak or a slot machine that doesn't pay out.

color up: Exchanging smaller denomination chips for larger denomination ones, often done in poker tournaments as the blinds and antes increase.

Come Bet: A wager placed on the Come Line in craps. It follows the same rules as the wager on the Pass Line except it is placed after the point has been established.

Come Line: The area on a craps table where the Come Bets are placed.

come out roll: The first roll of the dice or the first roll after a point has been made in craps. This roll establishes the point.

crap out: Rolling a Craps (two, three, or 12) on the come-out roll.

craps: A casino game of rolling dice. It is also a term for rolling a 2, 3, or 12.

credit button: A button in video poker that allows the player to bank coins won as credits and to use the credits to play without depositing more money.

crew: The dealers working a craps game.

cycle: In video poker it's the statistically predicted average number of hands dealt per top jackpot, which is usually a royal flush.

cut card: A hard plastic card used to cut the deck.

dealer: A casino employee who deals the various games.

dice: Two or more die.

die: Singular for dice, a six-sided cube, usually with each side numbered 1–6.

Don't Come Bet: A bet placed on the Don't Come Bar. Same rules as the Don't Pass Line except it is placed after the Come Out Roll.

Don't Pass Bet: A bet, placed prior to the Come Out Roll, that a 7 will be rolled before a point is repeated.

Don't Pass Line: Area of the table where the Don't Pass bets are placed. Also known as the Back Line.

double down: In blackjack, to double the original wager after the first two cards are dealt in exchange for receiving only one more card.

dozen bet: A bet on twelve numbers in roulette, i.e. 1–12, 13–24, or 25–36.

draw button: Allows video poker players to draw up to five new cards.

drop box: On a gaming table, the box that serves as a repository for cash, markers, and chips.

edge: The casino's advantage over the player in any game. Also known as house edge.

even money: A bet that pays you back the same amount you wagered, plus your original wager—a payoff of 1-1.

expected win rate: A percentage of the total amount of money wagered that you can expect to win or lose over time. In just about every casino game, the house has an edge meaning only the casino has an expected win rate.

face cards: The King, Queen, or Jack of each suit.

five number bet: A bet only possible on the double zero roulette games, which includes double 0s, 0, 1, 2, 3 and has the highest house edge of 7.89 percent.

flat top: A slot machine whose jackpot is always a fixed amount, as opposed to a progressive jackpot that increases with each bet until it pays off.

flush in poker: A hand consisting of five cards of one suit.

fold: In poker, when a player declines to call a previous bet and drops out of the hand.

four of a kind: Four cards of the same rank. Also known as quads.

full house: In poker, a hand consisting of a three of a kind and a pair.

full pay: In video poker, it's usually the best payoff schedule offered for a particular game.

hand: Refers to the cards that you hold, or to everything that happens in a card game between shuffles of the deck.

hit: To take another card.

hole card: A face-down card. In blackjack, the dealer's one down card or in poker, each player will have his own down cards.

horn bet: A one-roll bet that combines the 2, 3, 11, and 12.

inside bet: A bet in roulette on a single number or any combination of numbers.

insurance: A side bet in blackjack that's offered when the dealer's upcard is an Ace. If the dealer has a blackjack, the bet is paid 2-1. If the dealer does not, the insurance bet loses.

Let It Ride: A type of poker game.

loose/tight slots: A loose slot indicates a machine with a higher payout over a period of time. Conversely, tight slots have a lower payout over a period of time and thus have a higher advantage over the player.

mini-baccarat: A scaled-down version of baccarat, played with fewer players, dealers, and formality but following the same rules as baccarat.

odds: Ratio of probabilities or the amount a bet pays, for example 2-1, 3-2.

off: Bets that are not working.

on tilt: A bad reaction to an unlucky hand resulting in uncontrolled wild play.

one-roll bets: Wagers that win or lose depending on the next roll of the dice.

outside bets: Roulette bets located on the outside part of the layout. They involve betting 12 to 18 numbers at one time and result in a lower payout.

paint: A Jack, Queen, or King; picture card; face card.

palette: The tool (usually a long, flat wooden baton) used in the baccarat game to move cards on the table.

pair: Any two cards that have the same rank such as 4-4. Pairs can be split in blackjack and played as two hands.

pass: In card games, to not bet.

Pass Line: The area where a Pass Line Bet is placed.

Pass Line Bet: A wager made prior to the Come Out Roll that a point will repeat.

pat: In draw poker, a hand that does not need any new cards after the draw. In blackjack, an unbusted hand worth at least 17 points.

payline: The line on a slot machine window on which the symbols from each reel must line up. Slot machines can have as many as eight paylines, although most have only one.

payoff: The return or payback the player receives for her wager if she wins.

payoff odds: The form of odds that are conventionally posted in the casinos. Payoff odds specify how much a winning wager will be paid for each wager or chip that was bet. The casinos post the payoff odds in terms of the number of chips won relative to the number of chips bet.

payout: The amount of money paid out to you as a win.

payout percentage: The percent of each dollar played in a video or slot machine that the machine is programmed to return to the player. Payback percentage is stated in terms of 100 percent minus the house edge. For example, if the house edge is 5.6 percent, then the payback percentage is 94.4.

payout table: A posting somewhere on the front of a slot or video poker machine that tells you what each winning hand will pay for the number of coins or credits played.

pigeon: An uninformed or poor gambler.

pit: An area of a casino in which a group of table games are arranged, where the center area is restricted to dealers and other casino personnel.

pit boss: A supervisor who oversees a gaming area. Usually he supervises more than one table at the same time.

pit manager: A pit manager is in charge of all the table games, enforcing casino policy. She deals with any problems that may arise during the shift where a crucial decision must be made that may lead to a customer being dissatisfied or angry.

player: A person wagering money at a casino game.

playing the rush: Being aggressive in the midst of a good winning streak. A blackjack player playing the rush increases the size of his wager to take advantage of what he believes is a favorable deck.

point (the point): The number that is established on the Come Out Roll in craps. Only place numbers (4, 5, 6, 8, 9, 10) can become the point. The shooter will attempt to repeat throwing the point before throwing a 7 in order to win that round of betting.

pot: In a poker game, the amount of money that accumulates in the middle of the table as each player antes, bets, and raises. The pot goes to the winner of the hand.

press a bet: Adding the winnings over the current bet, to let it ride.

progressive: A slot machine whose potential jackpot increases with each coin that is played. When the progressive jackpot finally hits, the amount resets to the starting number.

Punto Banco: European name for baccarat; *punto* means "player" and *banco* means "bank."

push: A tie hand between a dealer and a player.

quads: In poker, four of a kind.

rack: A plastic container in which you can transport and count large-denominational coins, slot machine tokens, and casino plastic chips.

rake: The money that the casino charges for each hand of poker. It is usually a percentage (5–10 percent) or flat fee that is taken from the pot after each round of betting.

RFB: Room, food, and beverage.

RNG: A random number generator. A computer-generated method of randomly assigning the outcome of a result in a slot machine or video game.

royal flush: A hand consisting of an Ace, King, Queen, Jack, and Ten, all of the same suit. This is the best possible hand in poker.

session: A length of time playing any casino game.

seven-out: Rolling a 7 after the point has been established in craps, thus losing the bet.

shoe: Device used for holding and dispensing playing cards to be dealt and accommodating a number of decks at once. Used primarily in blackjack.

shooter: The person rolling the dice in craps.

snake eyes: When you roll a 2 in craps, it is called snake eyes—eyes because they look like eyes, snake because they are bad news (for the shooter).

soft hand: A hand in blackjack that contains an Ace counted as 11. It's soft because a player can always take another card and count the Ace as 1.

split bet: A combination bet across two numbers on the inside of the roulette table.

spot: Any number from 1 to 80 that a player selects on a keno ticket. It also refers to the number of numbers that are marked on a ticket.

stand: To refrain from taking another card.

stickman: The craps dealer who calls the numbers rolled and controls the stick.

suit: Any one of the four types of cards: clubs, diamonds, hearts, or spades.

surrender: In blackjack, to give up half your bet for the privilege of not playing out a hand.

tapping out: Losing one's entire gambling bank-roll and thus having to stop playing.

three of a kind: In poker, three cards of the same rank.

toke: Chips given by players to the dealers as tips.

upcard: The dealer's face-up card in blackjack.

vig., vigorish: The house advantage.

wager: Any bet.

whale: A very high roller.

working: A dice term meaning that the bets are in place.

Our Casino Picks

We have listed casinos that we believe offer great comp values. We took into account promotions, player's rewards, amenities, comfort, and convenience. Promotions change on a regular basis, so be sure to check out each casino's website for the latest and greatest deals.

Please note that not every casino was visited or researched. A casino's absence on this list should not be interpreted to mean that a casino does not offer great comp values.

Las Vegas

Arizona Charlie's—Decatur
740 S. Decatur Blvd.
Las Vegas, Nevada 89107
1-800-342-2695
www.azcharlies.com

Comments: Great breakfast deals in Sourdough Café. When you join the slot club, you can be reimbursed for your total day's losses (up to $100) the first day you play. In addition, earn extra points during your first two days of slot play under their Mystery Multiplier program.

Bally's Las Vegas
3645 Las Vegas Blvd. South
Las Vegas, Nevada 89109
1-800-7-BALLYS
www.ballyslv.com

Comments: Part of Harrah's Family. Centrally located in the heart of the Strip.

Bellagio
3600 Las Vegas Blvd. South
Las Vegas, Nevada 89109
1-888-987-6667
www.bellagioresort.com

Comments: High-end casino with top of the line restaurants and amenities.

Binion's Gambling Hall and Hotel
128 E. Fremont Street
Las Vegas, Nevada 89101
1-800-937-6537
www.binions.com

Comments: Binion's has built a long-standing reputation as catering to the serious gambler. Offers single-deck blackjack games and has a great coffee shop.

Boulder Station Hotel & Casino
4111 Boulder Highway
Las Vegas, Nevada 89121
1-800-981-5577
www.stationcasinos.com

Comments: Great promotional giveaways for joining slot clubs. Buffet discounts with slot club card.

Caesars Palace
3570 Las Vegas Blvd. South
Las Vegas, Nevada 89109
1-800-634-6001
www.caesars.com

Comments: High-end casino centrally located on the Strip. Houses large, upscale shopping mall and is part of the Harrah's family.

Circus Circus Hotel & Casino
2880 Las Vegas Blvd. South
Las Vegas, Nevada 89109
www.circuscircus.com
1-800-634-3450

Comments: Family oriented casino with plenty of games for kids. Free circus acts throughout the day.

Ellis Island Casino
4178 Koval Lane
Las Vegas, Nevada 89109
702-733-8901
www.ellisislandcasino.com

Comments: Hosts one of the best dinner deals in all of Las Vegas—a steak dinner for $4.95. You won't find it on the menu, though. You have to ask for it.

Four Queens Hotel & Casino
202 Fremont Street
Las Vegas, Nevada 89101
1-800-634-6045
www.fourqueens.com

Comments: A gambler's casino that offers great comp values and single-deck blackjack games. An added bonus is the inclusion of a couple of great restaurants on site and some real food values.

Golden Gate Hotel & Casino
One Fremont Street
Las Vegas, Nevada 89101
1-800-426-1906
www.goldengatecasino.com

Comments: Old-time downtown hotel and casino offering 99-cent shrimp cocktails.

The Golden Nugget
129 E. Fremont Street
Las Vegas, Nevada 89101
1-800-634-3403
www.goldennugget.com

Comments: A refurbished hotel at Fremont Street rates.

Luxor Las Vegas
3900 Las Vegas Blvd. South
Las Vegas, Nevada 89119
1-800-288-1000
www.luxor.com

Comments: At the southern end of the Strip, this pyramid-shaped hotel casino is one of the more reasonably priced themed Vegas properties.

Mandalay Bay
3950 Las Vegas Blvd. South
Las Vegas, Nevada 89109
1-877-632-7000
www.mandalaybay.com

Comments: Features a beach with pool that resembles the surf.

MGM Grand Hotel Casino
3799 Las Vegas Blvd. South
Las Vegas, Nevada 89109
1-800-929-1111
www.mgmgrand.com

The Mirage
3400 Las Vegas Blvd. South
Las Vegas, Nevada 89109
www.themirage.com
1-800-627-6667

Comments: The volcano outside with its scheduled eruptions was one of the first big outdoor attractions in Las Vegas.

Monte Carlo Resort & Casino
3770 Las Vegas Blvd. South
Las Vegas, Nevada 89109
1-800-311-8999

Comments: Upscale casino with plenty of amenities.

New York–New York Hotel & Casino
3790 Las Vegas Blvd. South
Las Vegas, Nevada 89109
1-800-693-6763
www.nynyhotelcasino.com

Comments: Features replicas of such New York institutions as the Statue of Liberty and the Empire State Building. Part of MGM Mirage family of casinos.

The Orleans Hotel & Casino
4500 W. Tropicana Avenue
Las Vegas, Nevada 89103
1-800-ORLEANS
www.orleanscasino.com

Comments: Family oriented with bowling lanes and movie theater. The Orleans is proximate to the Strip but more affordable. Shuttle service is offered to the Strip.

Palace Station Hotel & Casino
2411 West Sahara Avenue
Las Vegas, Nevada 89102
1-800-544-2411
www.palacestation.com

Comments: Daily buffet prices and great promotional giveaways for joining their slot club.

The Palms
4321 Flamingo Road
Las Vegas, Nevada 89103
1-800-942-7777
www.thepalmslasvegas.com

Comments: Upscale hotel and casino with great buffet deals.

Paris Casino Resort
3655 Las Vegas Blvd. South
Las Vegas, Nevada 89109
1-800-BON-JOUR
www.parislasvegas.com

Comments: More affordable choice of upscale hotels in the heart of the Strip.

Planet Hollywood (formerly Aladdin Hotel & Casino)
3667 Las Vegas Blvd. South
Las Vegas, Nevada 89109
1-866-919-7472
www.aladdincasino.com

Comments: Great promotional values for joining player's club.

Rio Suites Hotel & Casino
3700 W. Flamingo Road
Las Vegas, Nevada 89103
1-800-PLAY-RIO
www.playrio.com

Comments: Upscale all-suite hotel with one of the best buffets in town. Current home of the World Series of Poker.

Sam's Town Hotel & Gambling Hall
5111 Boulder Highway
Las Vegas, Nevada 89122
1-800-897-8696
www.samstown.com

Comments: Off-the-Strip hotel and casino catering to locals and more serious gamblers. Discounts on buffets for holders of slot club cards.

Santa Fe Station Hotel & Casino
4949 North Rancho Drive
Las Vegas, Nevada 89130
1-866-767-7770
www.stationcasinos.com

Comments: One of the Station casino family properties that offers a cash play for signing up for the slot club.

Treasure Island
3300 Las Vegas Blvd. South
Las Vegas, Nevada 89109
1-800-944-7444
www.treasureisland.com

Comments: Located in the heart of the Strip at slightly better prices.

Tropicana Resort & Casino
3801 Las Vegas Blvd. South
Las Vegas, Nevada 89109
1-888-826-8767
www.tropicanalv.com

Comments: Giveaway promotions for signing up for their player's card include free T-shirts and show tickets when you begin to play. The Tropicana also offers slot promotions where you can earn extra comps playing their Lucky $20. Free coupon book available as well.

The Venetian Resort Hotel Casino
3355 Las Vegas Blvd. South
Las Vegas, Nevada 89109
1-888-283-6423
www.venetian.com

Comments: Upscale hotel and casino featuring all-suite rooms and top of the line amenities.

Wynn Las Vegas
3145 Las Vegas Blvd. South
Las Vegas, Nevada 89109
1-888-320-WYNN
www.wynnlasvegas.com

Comments: Las Vegas' newest upscale resort featuring a five-story waterfall.

Atlantic City

Atlantic City Hilton Casino Resort
Boston Avenue and the Boardwalk
Atlantic City, New Jersey 08401
1-800-257-8677
www.hiltonac.com

Comments: Right on the beach at the southern end of Atlantic City, this resort is a little quieter than others.

Bally's Atlantic City
Park Place and the Boardwalk
Atlantic City, New Jersey 08401
1-800-772-7777
www.ballysac.com

Comments: Part of the Harrah's family of properties.

Borgata Hotel Casino and Spa
One Borgata Way
Atlantic City, New Jersey 08401
1-866-692-6742
www.theborgata.com

Comments: The crown jewel of Atlantic City, this upscale resort has spurred an Atlantic City renaissance. By raising the bar with first-class amenities and fine restaurants, many of Atlantic City's other casinos are quickly following suit.

Caesars Atlantic City
2100 Pacific Avenue
Atlantic City, New Jersey 08401
1-800-443-0104
www.caesarsac.com

Comments: Part of the Harrah's family of casinos, this upscale property just opened an extravagant restaurant and shopping mecca over the beach on the Pier at Caesars. Total rewards-hidden jackpot promotion for all card holders.

Harrah's Casino Hotel
777 Harrah's Boulevard
Atlantic City, New Jersey 08401
1-800-2-HARRAH
www.harrahs.com

Comments: Located in the marina section, room rates are more reasonable than most of the other properties.

Resorts Atlantic City
1133 Boardwalk
Atlantic City, New Jersey 08401
1-800-336-6378
www.resortsac.com

Comments: New hotel tower recently added.

Showboat Casino-Hotel
801 Boardwalk
Atlantic City, New Jersey 08401
1-800-621-0200
www.harrahs.com

Comments: New Blues/Jazz theme. Part of Harrah's family of casinos.

Tropicana Casino & Resort
Brighton Avenue and the Boardwalk
Atlantic City, New Jersey 08401
1-800-THE-TROP
www.tropicana.net

Comments: Newly refurbished "The Quarter" section is one of the nicest restaurant/shop areas in the city.

Trump Marina Hotel Casino
Huron Avenue and Brigantine Blvd.
Atlantic City, New Jersey 08401
1-800-777-1177
www.trumpmarina.com

Comments: Good slot-clubs promotions and part of Trump's trio of casinos in Atlantic City.

Trump Plaza Hotel and Casino
Mississippi Avenue and the Boardwalk
Atlantic City, New Jersey 08401
1-800-677-7378
www.trumpplaza.com

Comments: Trump's property in the heart of Atlantic City.

Trump Taj Mahal Casino Resort
Virginia Avenue and the Boardwalk
Atlantic City, New Jersey 08401
1-800-825-8888
www.trumptaj.com

Comments: Very good restaurants including a private club for player's rewards only.

Native American

Arizona

Harrah's AK Chin Casino Resort
15406 Maricopa Road
Maricopa, Arizona 85239
1-800-HARRAHS
www.harrahs.com

Comments: Large casino with great buffet deals and part of Harrah's family of casinos.

California

Harrah's Rincon Casino & Resort
333750 Valley Center Road
Valley Center, California 92028
1-877-777-2457
www.harrahs.com

Comments: Beautiful facility outside of San Diego with reasonable hotel prices. Part of Harrah's family of casinos.

Pechanga Resort and Casino
45000 Pechanga Parkway
Temecula, California 92592
1-877-711-2946
www.pechanga.com

Comments: One of the largest and nicest casinos in Southern California.

Thunder Valley Casino
1200 Athens Ave
Lincoln, California 95648
1-877-468-8777
www.thundervalleyresort.com

Comments: One of the largest and nicest casinos in Northern California. Part of the Station casino family of properties. Offers great daily buffets at low prices.

Connecticut

Foxwoods Resort Casino
Route 2
Mashantucket, Connecticut 06338
860-312-3000
www.foxwoods.com

Comments: The largest casino in the United States with something for everyone.

Mohegan Sun Casino
1 Mohegan Sun Boulevard
Uncasville, Connecticut 06382
860-862-8000
www.mohegansun.com

Comments: Not as large as Foxwoods but close by and offers first-rate amenities.

Florida

Seminole Hard Rock Hotel & Casino— Hollywood
1 Seminole Way
Hollywood, Florida 33314
1-866-502-7529
www.seminolehardrockhollywood.com

Comments: Large property with top of the line amenities.

Seminole Hard Rock Hotel & Casino—Tampa
5223 N. Orient Road
Tampa, Florida 33610
1-800-282-7016
www.hardrockhotelcasinotampa.com

Comments: Large property with top of the line amenities.

Idaho

Coeur D'Alene Casino Resort Hotel
U.S. Highway 95/P.O. Box 236
Worley, Idaho 83876
1-800-523-2464
www.cdacasino.com

Comments: Very nice property with reasonable room rates in a resort setting.

New Mexico

Sandia Resort & Casino
30 Rainbow Road NE
Albuquerque, New Mexico 87113
1-800-526-9366
www.sandiacasino.com

Comments: Large, full-service casino with terrific daily buffet deals.

New York

Turning Stone Casino Resort
5218 Patrick Road
Verona, New York 13478
1-800-771-7711
www.turning-stone.com

Comments: Large, full-service casino. Their hotel has plenty of suites for not much more money than their regular rooms.

Oklahoma

Choctaw Casinos
Seven different locations
1-800-788-2464
www.choctawcasinos.com

Comments: Seven locations throughout the state, this family of casinos offers plenty of ongoing promotions. Visit their website for latest offers.

Casino Nation—A Look Around the Country

Colorado

Colorado Central Station Casino
340 Main Street
Black Hawk, Colorado 80422
1-800-843-4753
www.coloradocentralstation.com

Comments: With lots of competition in the area, comps can be good.

Isle of Capri Casino
401 Main Street
Black Hawk, Colorado 80422
1-800-843-4753
www.isleofcapricasino.com

Comments: Sister property of Colorado Central Station.

Delaware

Delaware Park Racetrack & Slots
777 Delaware Park Boulevard
Wilmington, Delaware 19804
1-800-41-SLOTS
www.delpark.com

Comments: Best return rate of Delaware's three casinos. Doesn't have a hotel but nearby Christiana Hilton offers a Delaware Park discount.

Florida

Horizon's Edge Casino Cruises
200 N. Biscayne Boulevard
Miami, Florida 33131
305-523-2270
www.horizonsedge.com

Comments: 500-passenger ship sails out of Miami and buffet is included.

Illinois

Casino Queen
200 S. Front Street
E. St. Louis, Illinois 62201
1-800-777-0777
www.casinoqueen.com

Comments: Best payback percentage in Illinois with buffet discounts for slot club members.

Harrah's Joliet
150 N. Joliet Street
Joliet, Illinois 60432
1-800-HARRAHS
www.harrahs.com

Comments: Harrah's property in the Chicago area.

Indiana

Caesars Indiana
11999 Avenue of the Emperors
Elizabeth, Indiana 47117
1-888-766-2648
www.caesarsindiana.com

Comments: Part of Harrah's family of casinos.

Iowa

Harrah's Council Bluffs
One Harrah's Boulevard
Council Bluffs, Iowa 51501
1-800-HARRAHS
www.harrahs.com

Comments: Harrah's brand with good buffet deals.

Louisiana

Harrah's New Orleans
Canal Street
New Orleans, Louisiana 70130
1-800-HARRAHS
www.harrahs.com

Comments: The only land-based casino in
Louisiana not on a reservation is run by Harrah's.
Free parking for slot club members with minimum
play.

Michigan

MGM Grand Detroit Casino
1300 John C. Lodge
Detroit, Michigan 48226
1-877-888-2121
http://detroit.mgmgrand.com

Comments: The MGM Grand brand in the
burgeoning Detroit market. With plenty of competition, comps can be had.

Mississippi (Biloxi)

Beau Rivage
875 Beach Boulevard
Biloxi, Mississippi 39530
1-888-750-7511
www.beaurivageresort.com

Comments: Large hotel and casino with very reasonable room rates. Part of MGM Mirage family of casinos.

Grand Casino Resort Biloxi
265 Beach Boulevard
Biloxi, Mississippi 39530
1-800-HARRAHS
www.grandbiloxi.com

Comments: Harrah's property with plenty of slot promotions.

Hard Rock Hotel & Casino—Biloxi
777 Beach Boulevard
Biloxi, Mississippi 39530
228-374-ROCK
www.hardrockbiloxi.com

Comments: Check website for date of reopening.

Isle of Capri Casino & Hotel
151 Beach Boulevard
Biloxi, Mississippi 39530
1-800-843-4753
www.isleofcapricasino.com/Biloxi

Comments: Great promotions for slot club members including room discounts. Part of Isle of Capri chain.

Mississippi (Tunica)

Bally's Tunica
1450 Bally's Boulevard
Robinsonville, Mississippi 38664
1-800-382-2559
www.ballystunica.com

Comments: Good buffet deals and reasonable room rates.

Grand Casino Tunica
13615 Old Highway 61 North
Robinsonville, Mississippi 38664
1-800-946-4946
www.grandtunica.com

Comments: Part of Harrah's chain. Great room specials and check out its exclusive online e-mail promotions.

Horseshoe Casino & Hotel
1021 Casino Center Drive
Robinsonville, Mississippi 38664
1-800-303-7463
www.horseshoe.com

Comments: Part of Harrah's chain. Great buffet deals and reasonable room rates.

Missouri

Harrah's North Kansas City
One Riverboat Drive
N. Kansas City, Missouri 64116
1-800-HARRAHS
www.harrahs.com

Comments: Harrah's property.

Harrah's St. Louis
777 Casino Center Drive
Maryland Heights, Missouri 63043
1-800-HARRAHS
www.harrahs.com

Comments: Harrah's property.

Isle of Capri Casino
1800 E. Front Street
Kansas City, Missouri 64120
1-800-843-4753
www.isleofcapricasino.com

Comments: Part of Isle of Capri chain of casinos.

Pennsylvania

Harrah's Chester Casino & Racetrack
35 E. 5th Street
Chester, PA 19103
1-800-HARRAHS
www.harrahs.com

Comments: Located only about an hour from
Atlantic City, comps here are transferable to
Harrah's properties at the shore.

South Dakota

Gold Dust Gaming & Entertainment Complex
688 Main Street
Deadwood, South Dakota
1-800-456-0533
www.golddustgaming.com

Comments: Full-service property with great buffet
deals and reasonable room rates.

Around the World

Canada

Casino de Montreal
1, avenue du Casino
Montreal, Quebec
H3C 4W7
1-800-665-2274
www.casino-de-montreal.com

Comments: Has three sister casinos throughout Quebec.

Casino Niagara
5705 Falls Avenue,
Niagara Falls, ON
L2H 6T3
1-888-946-3255
www.casinoniagara.com

Comments: Wide range of aggressive slot promotions.

Casino Windsor
377 Riverside Drive East
Windsor, Ontario
N9A 7H7
1-800-991-7777
www.casinowindsor.com

Comments: Regular buffet specials.

Grand Casino
325 Southeast Marine Drive
Vancouver, British Columbia
Canada V5X 2T9
604-321-4402

Bahamas

Atlantis
Paradise Island, Bahamas
1-888-528-7155
www.atlantis.com

Comments: Periodic big prize slot and blackjack tournaments.

Crystal Palace Casino
Cable Beach Resorts & Crystal Palace Casino
Nassau, Bahamas
1-800-2-CASINO
www.cablebeachresorts.com

Comments: Everyone Wins! Promotions.

Caribbean

Aruba Marriott Resort and Stellaris Casino
L.G. Smith Boulevard #101
Palm Beach, Aruba
1-800-223-6388
www.marriott.com

Comments: Use Marriott rewards to stay. Has sister property the Renaissance on same island.

Excelsior Casino
J.E. Irausquin Boulevard 230
Palm Beach, Noord
Aruba, Dutch Caribbean
297-586-7777
www.excelsiorcasino.com

Appendix C

Additional Resources

Walking into a casino can be a daunting experience for the uninitiated. Even for more experienced gamblers, there are some useful guides out there to develop a better understanding of casino games. Here are some recommendations.

Recommended Books

Apostolico, David. *The Pocket Idiot's Guide to Tournament Poker*, Alpha Books, 2006. Okay, so I am biased. Tournament poker is one of the fastest growing and most popular games offered in most casinos. With low buy-ins, a player can get a lot of action for little cost. This book will give you everything you need to know to get started and get in the game.

Bourie, Steve. *American Casino Guide, 2007 Edition*, Casino Vacations, 2007. A valuable, in-depth resource for researching casinos throughout America. While not big on comp advice, this book does contain over 100 pages of coupons for casinos throughout the country, providing you a jumpstart on freebies. If you are headed to Las Vegas, the coupons alone are more than worth the cost of the book.

Ford, James Harrison. *How to Gamble at the Casinos Without Getting Plucked like a Chicken*, El Paso Norte Press, 2004. One of the best books out there at explaining a player's chances of winning at various casino games.

Paymer, Dan. *Video Poker: Optimum Play, 2nd Edition*, Conjelco, 2004. A comprehensive guide to video poker.

Rubin, Max. *Comp City: A Guide to Free Casino Vacations, 2nd Edition*, Huntington Press, 2001. An amusing book that offers some valuable insights into the comp system of casinos. Read with caution, however, as some of the advice may be outside of your comfort zone.

Scott, Jean. *The Frugal Gambler, 2nd Edition*, Huntington Press, 2005. The Queen of Comps offers a wide range of advice. A good book for low rollers.

Wong, Stanford, and Susan Spector. *The Complete Idiot's Guide to Gambling like a Pro, Fourth Edition*, Alpha Books, 2005. A comprehensive guide to just about every game offered in a casino. The authors take the reader step by step through the rules of play, the house edge, and the optimum playing strategy. Written in an entertaining and easy-to-understand manner, this book is an essential treatise for casino gaming.

Online Resources

There are a number of websites out there dedicated to various aspects of casinos and gambling. Do a Google search to find one you like. Here are a few that I recommend.

www.atlanticcitynj.com   One of the best online sources for planning a trip to Atlantic City.

www.lasvegasadvisor.com   A comprehensive look at everything Las Vegas, including some tips on games and comps.

www.readybetgo.com   Filled with expert columns on every major casino game, this site also offers some valuable tips on comps.

Help for Problem Gamblers

Gambling is a fun and recreational activity for the great majority of people who enter a casino. They recognize that they are likely to lose money in the long run, and they only wager what they have put aside for leisure activities. The money spent is no different than money spent on movies, golf, or bowling.

Unfortunately, there will always be some people who bet more than they can afford to lose and become problem gamblers. Gambler's Anonymous and other organizations exist to offer these people help. However, for the person who feels that his gambling might be getting out hand, following are a few examples of warning signs to consider.

- If gambling becomes the focus of your life.
- If you borrow funds with which to gamble.
- If gambling interferes with your family or business obligations.
- If you feel compelled to gamble and unable to stop.
- If you experience a euphoria from gambling stronger than anything else.
- If you find yourself gambling or betting on anything, no matter how insignificant.

If you find you have experienced any or all of these conditions, you may need help.

If you believe you may have a gambling problem, the following organizations can provide help:

The National Council on Problem Gambling
1-800-522-4700
www.ncpgambling.org

Gambler's Anonymous
213-386-8789
www.gamblersanonymous.org

Gam-Anon (Helps spouses, family, and loved ones of problem gamblers)
718-352-1671
www.gam-anon.org

Index

Q-R

S